SAVE OUR GAME

What's wrong with hockey training today and how to fix it

By Josh Levine

In memory of my father, Joel Eric Levine

Table of Contents

Introduction	5
Chapter 1: To Specialize Early or Not – The Great Debate	9
Chapter 2: Off-Ice Training	57
Chapter 3: Leadership, Character, and Team Training in Hockey	89
Chapter 4: On-Ice Training Sample Drills	104
Chapter 5: Agility Training Sample Drills	124

DISCLAIMER

Readers should consult with a doctor or appropriate healthcare professional equivalent prior to starting a new training program. All advice in this book is meant only for educational purposes. Readers should engage in exercise under the close supervision of a professional physical trainer. The author of this book disclaims all responsibility for injury to persons or property consequent to embarking upon the exercises or training advice herein described. Further, the author shall in no event be held liable to any party for any direct, indirect, punitive, special, incidental or other consequential damages arising directly or indirectly from any use of this material, which is provided "as is", and without warranties. The author makes no representation or warranties with respect to the accuracy, applicability, or completeness of the contents of this book.

Introduction

I grew up playing hockey for the Jefferson Jaguars in Bloomington, Minnesota. The city and state prided themselves, as they continue to do today, in their rich hockey traditions. Hockey was more than a sport – it was a lifestyle. Hockey was where I grew up, made friends, and learned life lessons. The Jefferson hockey association was more than a sports club too. It was a community. Families lived near each other, players hung out at teammates' homes, and there were parent socials. At the time, I didn't realize how special the experience was.

After graduating from high school I played one year in the United States Hockey League in Green Bay, Wisconsin. By the time I arrived in Green Bay, I didn't want to be there. I wanted to start my studies at Princeton University, where I was recruited to play hockey, rather than wait another season. By the end of my year in the USHL I was injured and the passion I once had for the game was all but extinguished. I finally decided to quit because if the game wasn't fun, it wasn't worth it. When I decided to end my career, I dove into a different area of my life that I have an overwhelming passion for, and that is physical training. I eventually started an athletic training company called The Fortis Academy.

The foundation of my knowledge and passion for this business came from one man – Jack Blatherwick. Jack is an eccentric thinker and an outside-the-box innovator who didn't adhere to the rules of athletic training that many trainers espoused. Although he only trained me for one year, the concepts he taught me were invaluable.

As an athletic trainer I became involved in youth sports in a way that I hadn't been since a young child. It was obvious that the game I had grown up with had changed and for the worse. Young players were being pressured by parents, coaches, and trainers to practice more, train more, and sacrifice more. The culture of high stakes professional sports was being mimicked at the youngest levels of youth hockey. More and more players, as a result, were becoming burnt out psychologically. Many more played without any passion. It hurt to see partially because it reminded me, in many ways, of my upbringing in the sport.

When I hit my early teens many of my peers were training year-round. I felt compelled to train more as well. If they were doing all this training, then I needed to do it too. At such a young age, more meant better. I didn't think about the consequences. Eventually, I think all the training and constant focus on hockey ruined the game for me. I specialized too early and never fully recovered. I still enjoyed the game, but what was missing was the drive and passion. I didn't have the overwhelming desire to get to the rink like I used to. After all, I was there nearly all the time. The constant presence of hockey in my life de-sensitized my passion for the game.

What also reminded me of my playing days were the many injuries I saw among youth athletes. Young hockey players would get injured and the first question always pertained to how quickly they could get back on the rink. Since the "more is always better" philosophy reigned supreme (as it continues to), parents saw the loss in athletic gains a bigger risk than the possibility for re-injury. Further, since youth athletes were practicing so much they were getting overuse injuries. This happened to me too. I played and trained so much that my body broke down, slowly and over the course of many years, but eventually this overuse caused injuries.

As an athletic trainer I was now in a position to see the problem and work toward changing it. What I quickly realized, however, was that no matter how many parents I spoke with or seminars I put on, the game I loved wouldn't change for the better unless I could reach a majority of parents, players, and coaches. The incentives for a profit-maximizing hockey program severely outweigh those of community associations or businesses that favor less hockey at the younger ages. For every minute I spoke in defense of rest, recovery, and the value of multi-sport athletes, it seemed like AAA programs and trainers were able to promote their message and philosophy for an hour.

Ultimately, I realized that I needed to put the knowledge I had on hockey training into a book. I don't claim to know everything or always assume I'm right. However, I do know that the hockey culture we have today is destroying young athlete's futures not only in the game of hockey, but also in other areas of life. I see first-hand the damage that too much hockey can have on a young hockey player's academic, social, emotional, and athletic abilities.

In this book, I aim to de-mystify the myths and provide parents, coaches, and players with the knowledge necessary to adequately evaluate hockey training programs. The first chapter in this book is the most important. It details the research that I think demonstrates the folly of year-round hockey for youth athletes. I hope that this research and the arguments I make also force parents, players, and coaches to think outside the game.

The second chapter of this book details my hockey training philosophy. In chapters four and five I have included some on and off-ice drills for reference. However, the goal of this book is not to tell players exactly what to do for training. The goal is to provide a basic philosophical framework which parents, players, and coaches can use to evaluate training programs. Finally, I firmly believe elements missing in hockey training programs today are character, leadership, and teamwork. In the third chapter, I detail these life principles that help people become successful in all areas of life. Too often hockey has taken the unfortunate role in degrading young athletes' values, teaching them selfishness over teamwork, entitlement over humility, and whining over effort. If we utilize hockey to teach values and build character, athletes playing hockey today will be far better off tomorrow. Let's change the tide and save our game.

To Specialize Early or Not – The Great Debate

Chapter 1

Current Trends

It's complicated. That's a common phrase I hear when talking with parents about hockey training and the multitude of hockey program options they have for their players. They're right, too. When parents first enter the world of hockey they are bombarded with information about the game. Some parents advocate for one training program's effectiveness, and others vehemently oppose it. What parents will almost unanimously be told, however, is in order for their son or daughter to become a great hockey player, they will have to spend a lot of money, shuttle their young hockey players from one game to the next, and be prepared to sacrifice. Increasingly, the prevailing wisdom among parents and hockey trainers is that year-round hockey is "normal." To think otherwise is to jeopardize an athlete's future in the game. Parents can be risk averse, so when given the option often the decision is to have the athlete play more and train longer than to do the opposite. It seems like the safer option. As one parent stated in a *New York Times* article about youth sport time commitments, if my son "doesn't get to play soccer in high school because he didn't get involved early, then the person who would potentially be harmed down the road is my son[1]." This father went on to state, "the one thing I won't do is make my kid's future a test case[2]." The irony is his child's athletic future is a test case – one I'll explain and provide data to support in the following pages.

Hockey parents utilize this line of reasoning all the time. When I issued a survey to parents and asked them if year round training was necessary, the responses were extraordinary. One parent wrote, "Unfortunately yes. As much as I would prefer my son to play baseball all summer, all of his peers are playing AAA[3]." Another wrote, "I feel year round hockey has become the only way most players can get the exposure to play for competitive high school programs[4]." There is significant pressure on parents to have their players train year round. If I were a parent, I would feel this pressure too. One of the biggest issues hockey parents must wrestle with is the decision of whether or not their child should specialize in hockey. There's always someone telling a parent his or her hockey player needs to skate more. Unfortunately, many parents need more information about hockey training to be able to ascertain whether or not their player should specialize in hockey or play multiple sports.

There's also the problem of culture shock. When parents move from an area where hockey is not popular to an area where hockey is the only thing people seem to talk about, they may feel like they are on a different planet. Hockey has a very unique culture, and it can be overwhelming at first. What parents, no matter their level of expertise, can see and understand is that most everybody is playing year round. The best players *seem* to be in the most elite AAA programs and time intensive leagues. Parents tend to confuse the correlation between playing AAA hockey and developing elite hockey players with causation. Those programs don't necessarily cause players to develop into elite athletes; in most cases, they are just better at recruiting elite talent

Coaches are also propagating the myth that hockey players need to train year round. One parent responding to an online survey I posted stated a coach had implied and/or overtly indicated, "In order for my child to continue to maximize his potential...he needs to train and play year round hockey[5]." A herd like mentality has shifted the way our youth play hockey. Parents, coaches, and most players themselves believe the myth that hockey players must train year round if they want to be "A" players. They believe, quite wrongly, that more is better and follow this logic: if we could only play hockey all year, all the time, we'd produce better hockey players.

What is Early Specialization?

Playing hockey year round with more tournaments, longer practices, and more travel is part of an increasingly disturbing trend toward sport specialization. This trend has seen younger and younger hockey athletes deciding to stop playing multiple sports in favor of *deliberately* practicing for hockey. There is also an increase in the intensity of games and practices in the youth hockey ranks. Many athletes play at least two seasons – the community winter leagues and the AAA leagues in the spring/summer. Some even play on two teams during one season.

A result of sport specialization is not simply a singular emphasis on one sport, but also a change in how athletes are training. Specialization also implies deliberate practice. It entails a rigid and scheduled practice routine that maximizes repetitions with disregard to the enjoyment of the players. When players are older, this is something they have to learn to do – to an extent.

Sport specialization is something any serious hockey player must consider at some point, but the decision doesn't need to be made by eight years old, as some coaches suggest. Instead of quitting other sports, athletes should be encouraged to play multiple sports, especially when they are young and can more easily learn different motor skills.

As athletes get older, a greater focus on a given sport makes sense. So too does increasing the quantity and proportion of deliberate practices. Although I do believe that even at older ages the functionality and applicability of deliberate practice to a game that is far from deliberate or planned can be overstated. Drills often restrict the parameters of the game to practice a given skill like shooting, stickhandling, or passing. While these drills are good and necessary, they often don't require an athlete to perform them under conditions similar to a game.

When athletes specialize in hockey, they should do this without giving up all other sport activities. For example, hockey players also should consider playing baseball or track in high school during the spring off season. Lacrosse, soccer, basketball, and football have important cross training advantages as well. The benefits of running 100 and 200 meter sprints in track are extremely important and useful for hockey players. Lacrosse, in addition to helping promote foot speed, can help hockey players improve their hand movements. Learning to stick-handle a lacrosse ball helps an athlete train the fine muscles in the wrists to make very precise movements. From these limited examples, it is easy to see how cross training is a very effective way to boost hockey performance. It's important to understand the effectiveness of sport specialization depends on the proper utilization of cross training. Perhaps more importantly, however, is the timing of when an athlete decides to specialize in one sport. The problem for most youth hockey athletes that I work with is not that they specialize in hockey, but that they do so at too young an age. If an athlete specializes too early, the consequences can be disastrous.

The American Academy of Pediatrics (AAP) has written that youth athletes should "specialize only after reaching the age of puberty" because these athletes "tend to be more consistent performers, have fewer injuries, and adhere to sports...longer than those who specialize early.[6]" In a position statement on sports specialization, The National Association for Sport and Physical Education wrote, "for young people under age 15, year round specialization in a single sport is more often associated with developmental risks than rewards[7]." Youth develop at different paces. Some reach puberty early while others are late bloomers. The problem with specializing prior to puberty, as the AAP and the National Association for Sport and Physical Education point out, is the risks are high. Overuse injuries, psychological problems, and physical development are all negatively affected by early specialization in sport prior to the onset of puberty.

Hockey is a Late Specialization Sport

Often, those who promote early specialization for team sports will cite research for sports like gymnastics, where the research leans more in favor of early specialization for elite development. Figure skating and diving also are considered "early specialization" sports. If the best gymnasts specialize early, shouldn't hockey, soccer, football, lacrosse, or basketball players do the same? One AAA program in Minnesota makes its arguments with this reasoning

> *"When you look at other skilled sports like gymnastics, figure skating or even the performing arts hockey is behind. These sports and the arts try and identify potential elite children at a young age and start their training early. When the athlete reaches the age of 15 they are world class or are well on their way. How do they do this? By using a focused methodology, including an incredible amount of quality repetition[8]"*

Unlike a hockey game, a gymnast's routine is planned out well in advance. A diver practices the same dive over and over again before performing it. Figure skaters know exactly what they will do before stepping on the ice. This is not the case in hockey or any other team sport! The situations are variable; an infinite amount of possibilities exist in the game of hockey. At one moment the puck can be moving down the ice toward the opponent's goal and in a fraction of a second the puck can change possession, forcing each player to react. A player's reaction to any change on the ice must take into consideration the position of the five opposing players and sometimes the opposing goalie as well as the reactions of teammates. The best players are able to predict the evolution of the game – to skate to where the puck will be instead of where it is. You can't practice this skill very well in a drill. It comes from creativity, athleticism, dynamic training, and perhaps most of all, lots of time simply playing the game in a no-pressure environment.

Clearly a sport like gymnastics is highly planned, making preparation for it quite different than for hockey. In addition to this difference, however, is the simple fact that gymnastics as well as figure skating and swimming lack the same type of physical contact that is present in hockey. And even without the physical contact, these sports face an alarming number of overuse injuries. Gymnastics might be one of the worst sports for overuse injuries, which makes citing it as a sport to emulate all the more ironic.

Dr. Jerry Dwek, M.D. conducted a study that looked into adolescent gymnasts arm, hand, and wrist injuries. Dr. Dwek stated, "these young athletes are putting an enormous amount of stress on their joints and possibly ruining them for the future[9]." He went on to state that the extent of injuries discovered in the subjects studied "are likely to develop into early osteoarthritis[10]." In some extreme cases, young gymnasts can injure themselves to the point of deformity. Some even require surgery to shorten their ulna bone because overuse injuries have led to "early fusion of the radial growth plate[11]."

In sports like gymnastics and figure skating, constant repetition of the exact same movement is needed to be successful. Hockey is different. While there is one proper way to skate and to perform essential skills, being able to conduct these movements is not a "silver bullet" for success in the game. Quality repetitions are needed to master skills like stickhandling, but they can't all be performed in a garage or during practice drills. Hockey is too variable a game. The best stickhandler in the world that can't read and react to the movements of others on the rink will find it hard to utilize his or her stickhandling skills effectively. At young ages, it is important to not limit athletes to monotonous practices filled with repetitious drills. Doing so can stunt the creativity and passion of a young player while simultaneously not providing the player with the opportunity to practice skills in a more game like environment.

The American Development Model (ADM) designed by USA Hockey clearly focuses on the distinction between sports like gymnastics and hockey. The ADM states, "As with other contact/collision sports, ice hockey is classified as a late specialization sport[12]." Comparing gymnasts and figure skaters to hockey players is misguided. First, although there is a greater consensus that gymnasts or figure skaters need to specialize early, there are risks already noted that should put some doubt into any reasonable parents head. Second, whereas gymnasts' careers peak early, hockey players continue to improve well beyond the onset of puberty. Dieter Hackfort and Gershon Tenenbaum, in their book *Essential Processes for Attaining Peak Performance*, write that "gymnasts peak earliest (15-17 years of age)" whereas those in team sports reach "peak performance between 21 and 35 years of age[13]."

In fact, consider that the "highest levels of performance for gymnasts are almost exclusively seen before biological maturation takes place[14]." A hockey scout watching fifteen-year-old hockey players play would not conclude they had reached their peak performance. The scout would be looking for potential and asking: "Does this player have the ability to develop further at the higher levels?" Any given fifteen-year-old could potentially peak a decade later. In hockey, puberty is a value-add. Going through puberty helps athletes become faster, bigger, and stronger. Those attributes help make a hockey player successful, but, unfortunately, they can have the opposite effect for a gymnast. The best gymnasts tend to be shorter than the average person because in that sport it is an advantage to be smaller and more compact.

The fact is, hockey is not an early specialization sport and it is dangerous for hockey players to replicate the training philosophy of a sport like gymnastics. In later chapters, I'll discuss the training methodologies to use with players. First, however, I think it is important to better understand why early specialization not only harms hockey players by increasing their risk of injury (physically and psychologically), but also by inhibiting their athletic development.

Arguments against Early Specialization

For several reasons, early specialization hurts the development of all athletes. Perhaps the most ironic consequence of early specialization is it hurts the athletic development of young athletes by reducing their athletic foundation. By introducing high stakes competition too early and limiting creativity, early specialization can destroy the fun nature of the game, and lead to the learning of improper form.

Secondly, early specialization comes with a higher risk of overuse injuries. These injuries often hold back the athletic potential of an athlete or can end a career altogether. Finally, early specialization increases the likelihood that a young athlete will become psychologically burned out and want to quit the game. The affects overuse injuries and burnout have on our young athletes can be hard to measure. Those affects that are strong enough to be identified, like a career ending injury or an athlete quitting the game, are just the tip of the iceberg. What about the athletes who are playing at 90 percent because their knees hurt or because they don't have the same passion for the game they once did? Early specialization comes with tangible and hidden costs.

Limits the Athletic Foundation of Young Athletes

The whole idea behind early specialization is more hockey practice equals better hockey players. This is a dangerous assumption. Athleticism is the basic foundation of any sport, but it can't be built on a small base. Athleticism is the synergy of multiple movements. Imagine a hockey player skating, handling the puck, reacting to the movements of opponents and teammates, anticipating the future movements of each, and making a split second decision to pass, shoot, skate, or stickhandle. By thinking of hockey this way (or any sport), it shows athleticism is much more than the ability to simply perform a task like passing. Athleticism requires a level of foresight, quick thinking, reaction, creativity, and speed that is hard to mimic in a drill. It's also hard to teach if parameters are created that shut out creativity.

By playing other sports, young athletes can learn a variety of different movements and skills that are overlapping. Catching a ball in baseball is a skill that translates to a defenseman working the boards in the offensive zone. The same is true for hockey players that learn lacrosse. Stickhandling is one skill used in both sports. Footwork in soccer and basketball helps with sports where quick agility movements in tight spaces are required. All sports help young athletes learn a variety of different movements. It's important to realize, too, as young athletes, they are capable of learning, memorizing, and executing different movements fairly quickly. Once a young athlete turns into a young adult, it becomes much harder to learn new skills.

In addition to helping learn new movements, playing more than one sport helps young athletes be more creative and able to respond to the infinitely diverse set of situations they may encounter on the ice rink. Reading situations and reacting to them is a hard skill to learn, but one that is best understood when an athlete can contextualize them in a variety of different situations and sports. One study conducted in 2004 had a group of sixth grade boys play ultimate frisbee and then team handball. The study noted "positive transfer" of tactical skills when "students moved from ultimate frisbee to team handball, particular in passing decisions and offensive support[15]." By playing other sports that utilize similar tactical strategies, athletes may be able to not only transfer those skills to another sport, but also obtain a quicker ability to read, recognize, and react to situations.

Finally, *a singular focus on hockey training increases the risk of developing specific weaknesses that are otherwise avoidable.* Take for instance a comparison between playing hockey and soccer. Hockey players perform a distinct set of movements; it's a leg intensive sport that requires a player to utilize leg power and speed from the squatting position. When hockey players stride out, they utilize their hip flexor muscles to return their leg to the starting position. Hockey requires hamstring strength as well but certainly not the same type of hamstring strength and endurance that is needed in soccer. That's why a hockey player that hits the soccer field in the summer may be quite sore the first few practices as muscles he or she hasn't used as vigorously in hockey strengthen. By playing both hockey and soccer an athlete becomes more well-rounded physically and mentally.

The game of hockey favors different types of movements over others too. For example, a hockey player might skate north/south the majority of the time, and only skate east/west during critical plays. The better the skater, the more he or she will be able to skate in any direction and in confined spaces. However, in a half-court 3-on-3 basketball game athletes are constantly changing direction and doing so in small spaces. Also, athletes in a half-court 3-on-3 game don't work at a top speed of 40 meters, whereas a hockey player wants to get down the ice fast enough for a break away (NHL rinks are 61 meters in length). By playing both sports (and still emphasizing one), a hockey player can cross train, become more athletic, and ultimately gain skills to become a great hockey player.

Introduces High Stakes Competition Too Early

The Canadian Long Term Athlete Development Program states, "sport research shows that rushing into competition frequently results in technical, physical, tactical, psychological and emotional short comings that hinder performance[16]." Yet, some still maintain that by introducing children to deliberate practice, intense game schedules, and year round competition, we can accelerate their development. Competition and games are good, right? Not necessarily. In fact, we know "premature competition actually detracts from performance and achievement[17]."

The reason premature competition hurts performance is analogous to trying to make a young athlete build muscle mass prior to puberty or learn calculus before being able to do simple mathematics. In the same way, premature competition introduces the young athlete to an environment where the athlete is not psychologically prepared. Young hockey players want to play the game. They don't want to be "working" out there for their parents or coaches. They want to have fun. If the pressure to perform reduces the passion for the game, which I believe it often does at young ages, then that pressure is producing athletes with unlocked potential. Passion is the number one ingredient to become a successful hockey player. Without it, it is impossible to succeed at elite levels. The other problem with introducing high stakes competition and placing such a heavy emphasis on hockey is that young children begin to self-identify with the sport. They see their self-worth, to a dangerous extent, as a reflection of their ability to play hockey.

Competition is important, and young hockey players need to learn what it means to truly exert "100 percent." But, keeping this in perspective, there isn't the same expectation for a seven-year-old to read with the same concentration and attentiveness as a college student. I've redefined my definition of what "100 percent" means as I learn how far I can actually push myself. If someone tried forcing me to work as hard as I know I can today when I was seven years old, I would have quit the sport because I wouldn't have learned the many definitions of hard work that came between then and now. There's a reason elementary school teachers move quickly through subjects and don't spend two hours focusing on one. Doing so would burn the students out, their focus would wane, and the rest of the teaching would be useless.

Premature competition also can be severely damaging because it doesn't allow athletes to fully develop at a given level. Jack Blatherwick, my ninth grade mentor, wrote an article titled, "The myth of leaving home and advancing quickly." In it he writes about the young and talented Freddy Adu who at age 14 stunned the soccer world with his skills and finesse. He joined the professional ranks, but in so doing never, as Blatherwick writes, "developed awareness, anticipation, creativity, poise, and mental toughness – the most important skills in every team sport[18]." Jack chastises our "hurry up society" that, due to reputation and status, would rather put a player on an A team before he or she is ready. Instead of dominating the B level, parents (perhaps more than their own children), have tended to demand their hockey player play on the very best team. Not only that, but they demand they win every game. So instead of playing, learning, and making mistakes, coaches at the youth levels are playing games just to win. This of course has a couple negative consequences.

First, instead of developing creative skills, athletes are pigeonholed. The scenario goes something like this: A coach might tell the player he or she is to be a defensive player; his or her goal is only to stop the other team from scoring. Under no circumstances should this player try to go on offense. It's too risky for the success of a youth regular season game. That logic is a prime example of what destroys young athletic careers. Instead of learning by making mistakes and eventually gaining new skills, they are pigeonholed into a position. They lose dynamic athleticism and play more like industrialized and manufactured athletes that can only perform pre-mediated movements. If winning comes at the expense of development at the youngest levels, is it really winning? There are still times during youth sports when a coach may want and need to make decisions that limit a given player's role on the ice for the betterment of the group. My point here is that we've taken this too far and that too often young hockey players never really get the chance to just *play* the game.

Second, by only concentrating on winning, young athletes aren't learning life lessons that will be more valuable to them later in life. They need to learn to play together, to play as a team – win or lose – and to have a competitive spirit they sustain amid trials and tribulations (not just whenever they're winning). Freddy Adu's story is sad and unfortunate. Yet, it is preventable. Blatherwick sums up this lost opportunity to develop an amazing American soccer player:

> *"Imagine, the most skillful soccer player in the country at age 14, stopped learning the game at age 15. He didn't get the chance to dominate 15-year-old games; he didn't play unstructured pick up soccer with his friends. He lost opportunities to develop confidence, poise, creativity, and playmaking abilities, simply because he didn't stay with his peers and "play" like a 15-year- old*[19]*."*

Teaches Improper Form

The primary reason early specialization does not work is because *repetitions make permanent, not perfect.* This is a simple principle every parent, player, and coach needs to understand. When a hockey player only plays hockey, that player repeats the same movements over and over again. The same set of muscles are worked and broken down, stressed, and fatigued.

A hockey player who skates too much will inevitably fatigue, and once fatigue sets in, the player will bend at the waist, not the knees. The player's stride shortens and he or she fails to keep the full blade on the ice. Instead of a smooth, clean stride, the player's stride becomes choppy. When a player skates with improper form, that form is being learned. That is why when athletes practice too much, it can be detrimental to their future success. The quality of repetitions matters just as much or more than the quantity. Hockey players can always relearn the proper technique, but it gets more and more difficult as the athlete ages. Just ask a hockey dad that can't skate; it would take a long time to teach him to skate, whereas a squirt or peewee level player learns in much less time.

Practicing too much can literally make an athlete a worse player by teaching the improper form, breaking down the muscles, and not allowing for sufficient rest and recovery.
Early specialization not only risks repeating movements in an incorrect manner, but it also creates the risk of repeating (even correctly) the same movements too often.

Imagine a weight lifter who goes into the weight room every day and only works his chest and biceps. He works hard. The competitions only focus on the chest and biceps so it makes sense he'd focus only on those muscle groups, right? Hopefully, the absurdity of this situation is clear. By training only the chest and biceps, the weight lifter would cause a lot of problems to his body. His chest would get too big relative to his back; his arms would have tiny triceps and big biceps. Eventually he'd get injured because his muscle growth would be disproportional. Secondary muscles used in the bench press like the triceps or deltoids would not get worked as intensely and their growth, relative to the chest, would be disproportional. In other words, a singular approach in training may help get short term gains quickly, but it will eventually create body distortions and neglect important muscle groups. Ultimately, this can lead to overuse injuries.

Increases Risk of Overuse Injuries

Athletes who specialize early risk not being able to maximize the gains they could reap from their young and formative years (prior to age 15 or so). Early specialization is a contributing factor to the increase in overuse injuries that are reaching epidemic levels. In fact, a lot of the overuse injuries seen today did not exist previously. A fact sheet on overuse injuries in young athletes created by Dr. Lyle Micheli, faculty member of the Division of Sports Medicine at Children's Hospital Boston states, "overuse injuries were once virtually unknown in young athletes[20]." It goes on to state that this all changed with the "emergence of organized sports and their emphasis on repetitive coaching drills, as well as the recent trend toward sports specialization in young athletes[21]." It is important to understand the real and dangerous risks associated with early specialization. The fact that the medical field has had to come up with new diagnoses of injuries previously unheard of is a disturbing, yet telling piece of information.

Stop Sports Injuries, an organization dedicated to raising awareness about the disastrous consequences of doing too much too early, writes the "number of youth injuries is reaching epidemic proportions and youth are experiencing overuse injuries at a younger and younger age[22]." Indeed, "up to half of the 3.5 million sports injuries suffered by kids and teens every year" are caused by overuse injuries[23]. What is most disturbing about overuse injuries is they are *almost entirely preventable*. Unfortunately, many parents and coaches involved in hockey aren't willing to understand the simple cure – rest and recovery.

These overuse injuries aren't just muscle strains or sprains. Overuse injuries are leading to career ending injuries like never seen before. Take, for example, Tommy Johns surgery. E. Lyle Cain, MD, the fellowship director for the American Sports Medicine Institute and coauthor of a study conducted by the American Orthopedic Society for Sports Medicine, stated, "before 1997 this surgery [Tommy Johns] was performed on only 12 of 97 patients who were 18 or younger (12 percent)[24]." However, in 2005, "62 of the 188 operations performed were on high school athletes[25]." Dr. James R. Andrews, a surgeon in Birmingham, Alabama, wrote in "Sports Illustrated", "I don't think epidemic is too strong a word. We're seeing kids hurt before they even have a chance to become athletes[26]." He's right. When young players have surgery in high school, they might not be taking themselves off the field completely, thanks to modern medicine, but they are losing very valuable training time. If a high school athlete undergoes an ACL surgery, that athlete will be out a minimum of six months, but probably won't start feeling great and training at 100 percent for 9 to 12 months later. An entire year of tremendous gains in athleticism are lost if a young athlete has to undergo surgery.

We are also seeing alarming increases in ACL injuries. Pediatric hospital records from 1999 to early 2011 found "155 tibial spine fractures, while there were 914 confirmed A.C.L. tears and 996 meniscus tears[27]." What also should be alarming for parents and athletes alike is the "incidence of A.C.L. tears increased by more than 11 percent per year[28]" during this period. Dr. J. Todd Lawrence, the principal researcher in this study has his suspicions as to why the alarming increase is occurring: "I think it's primarily because kids are out there trying to emulate professional athletes. You see these very young athletes playing sports at an extremely intense, competitive level. Kids didn't play at that level 20 years ago. They didn't play one sport year-round[29]." He's right, and the cure to the problem couldn't be simpler: rest.

The issue of overuse injuries in youth athletes is serious. It's something that needs to be addressed quickly – both so injuries are reduced and the skill and abilities of players are increased. Although young athletes may seem to bounce back from surgery pretty quickly the long-term effects of these injuries are still somewhat unknown. Arthritis is likely to increase in prevalence among this population as they age. Mark Hyman details the story of Christy Hammond, who after a series of surgeries and medical treatments, has been riddled with pain: "She can't recall a pain free day for nearly five years[30]." Now she can't "bike, swim, or work out at the gym[31]." Essentially, her life was altered significantly because of overuse injuries and the impression that surgery can work miracles. Modern medicine still has its limitations. The body can only take so much.

John H. Klippel, M.D., president and CEO of the Arthritis Foundation has issued a stark warning, "Today's young athletes may become tomorrow's osteoarthritis patients, unless parents and coaches take an active role in sports injury prevention[32]." The problem is surgery, although effective in the short term for getting athletes back onto the field, is not beneficial for young athletes' long term health. In fact, Dr. Scott Tashman in the "Pittsburg Post Gazette' stated, "When you have an ACL injury, your risk of arthritis increases dramatically[33]." He says 60 to 80 percent of those who suffer an ACL injury will develop arthritis within 10 years[34].

Specialization in one sport also leads to overuse injuries because it is physiologically harmful to the development of a young athlete. The constant use of the same muscle groups and movements can create repetitive stresses on joints and muscles that young athletes simply can't handle. Dr. James Hurley, an orthopedic surgeon who specializes in sports medicine, discussed in "Sports Illustrated Kids" the growing trend of overuse injuries:

> *"The culture of youth sports has changed tremendously. Because of this new culture of one sport athletes, we tend to see a lot more overuse injuries because they are stressing one part of their body all the time as opposed to participating in different sports where they're putting the stress on a different part of the body during different seasons[35]."*

Evidence seems to suggest that limiting the amount of competition in one sport actually helps improve the long term success of athletes. For example, the Women's Tennis Association (WTA) in the 1990s was concerned about its young players turning professional too early and the stress as well as negative ramifications from this trend. They instituted a rule that limited the amount of play based on age – as athlete's got older they were allowed to participate in more tournaments. When the WTA evaluated their rule 10 years later they found "players increased their career length by 43 percent, and premature retirements (players leaving the tour before age 21) declined from seven percent before the rule to less than one percent after its initiation[36]." Although this type of study does not indicate a causal relationship, it seems very plausible that one exists. Premature competition hinders the growth of an athlete by putting them in situations they may be ready for skill wise, but not in terms of their physical and psychological development. And unlike Freddy Adu, athletes need to learn to dominate play and be creative at younger levels before moving to the professional ranks where winning trumps development.

Increases the Risk of Psychological Burnout

Sports are mental exercises as much or more as they are physical exercises. When a young athlete gets burnt out, they won't progress. Furthermore, as I've already mentioned, passion is the number one ingredient necessary to reach elite performance and early specialization often destroys this passion.

Young hockey players who specialize early are more likely to run into issues of psychological and emotional burnout. Imagine this situation for yourself if you are a parent or coach. Even if you can't skate imagine that you can. Today you will practice for an hour and do dryland after the skate. Regardless of what you would like to do, we are going to do lots of repetitive drills. We will do this again tomorrow and the next day, and well, we will continue doing this until you can no longer play the game. Are you ready?

To put it into an adult context for parents and coaches: would you rather have autonomy and be intrinsically motivated at your job or have a boss that dictates to you every day what you need to do and how to do it?

When players take time off, they rejuvenate and become "hungrier" to get out on the ice. Coaches would rather have players that are pumped to play and energized, even if less skilled, than the talented players that don't care too much for the game.

Psychological burnout in youth hockey players is real, but to what extent? Young athletes can feel pressured to play and feel uncomfortable telling their parents they want to quit. Those players who ask to quit, and actually do, aren't the only ones thinking about it. Many young athletes are too afraid to tell their parents they don't want to play or would like to play less. They can easily see the emphasis our culture places on sports and the importance parents put on their youth player's success. In this environment, it is very difficult for young athletes to speak their mind.

For those athletes who continue to play, the negative effects of burnout are difficult to see. Players may not get burnt out to the point of quitting the game entirely, but they may lose the passion and desire they once had for the sport. The problem again is developmental. If we want to produce great players in any sport, the one ingredient that can't be taught or put into a drill is passion. Passion for competition is the most basic and necessary ingredient a player needs to be successful. Yet, early specialization puts players at risk of losing the very intangible quality needed to become a great athlete. We can't measure the loss of skills and ability from an athlete playing with 80 or 90 percent passion, but it certainly seems to be affecting some of today's young athletes.

How Hockey Players Should Train

Play Multiple Sports to Increase Athletic Foundation

Instead of specializing in basketball or hockey, athletes should play multiple sports. Hockey players should play as many different sports as possible when they are young. Wayne Gretzky, one of the greatest NHL hockey players in history, believes young athletes *need* to play multiple sports as well. He said,

> *"In youth hockey, in most cases, it's really important for kids to play other sports – whether it's indoor lacrosse or soccer or baseball. I think what that does is two things. One, each sport helps the other sport. And then I think taking time off in the off season that three or four month window – really rejuvenates kids so when they come back at the end of August, they're more excited. They think, 'All right, hockey's back. I'm ready to go*[37]*."*

Most young athletes want to play multiple sports. In fact, I don't know any true athlete who doesn't want to play different sports. They are fun, and by playing different sports, athletes learn new movements and acquire a more diverse range of athletic abilities. The ADM model by USA Hockey suggests, "specialization at an early age limits children from acquiring a broad spectrum of athletic movements and skills that may limit or put a cap on their overall athletic potential[38]." As Dr. Mark Lemos, an orthopedic surgeon and director of sports medicine at Lahey Clinic in Burlington stated, "multiple sports will benefit them [athletes] at all levels...even guys who play professional sports cross train[39]." Cross training is essential for building athleticism.

The ability to shoot a basketball, hit a baseball, throw a football and skate backwards in hockey are all different athletic abilities. At first glance, some movements athletes learn in one sport don't seem very applicable to another, but given further thought, it makes more sense.

Imagine a young student learning several languages instead of specializing in English. Many people learn two or more languages while growing up. As older students, they tend to learn another language quickly because they already learned several as young children, especially if the languages are similar. There are more parallels between learning languages and training for sports. Some psychologists have wondered whether attempting to learn two languages at once causes a deficit in both. Sounds familiar? It's the same question parents have about sports: Will a child playing multiple sports be mediocre at them all and never elite in one? Researchers at Dartmouth University's Department of Psychology and Brain Sciences found "children...exposed to two languages from a very early age...will essentially grow as if there were two monolinguals housed in one brain[40]." In fact, learning a couple languages early in life is better than simply learning one. As Therese Sullivan Caccavale, President of the National Network for Early Language Learning (NNELL), said, "children who learn a foreign language beginning in early childhood demonstrate certain cognitive advantages over children who do not[41]."

Like children who learn multiple languages at a young age, athletes can learn multiple and varied skills like shooting a basketball, stickhandling with a hockey puck, and swinging a golf club. Therefore, athletes who have a broad array of motor skills as opposed to those who decided to specialize will more easily learn more complex movements. Athletes who can stick handle a lacrosse ball may more quickly learn new hockey stickhandling techniques than athletes who didn't play lacrosse. Many studies have shown that playing a variety of sports is conducive to the development of elite athletes. One study found "many international athletes have not progressed through 'linear' sport careers exclusively within one discipline, but have practiced multiple sports during childhood and adolescence[42]."

Take two athletes that are genetically identical in terms of athletic potential. Suppose one athlete plays hockey, soccer, baseball, and golf while the other athlete only plays hockey. Now, who would make a better basketball player? Which one will learn new skills faster?

Playing multiple sports not only increases the athletic foundation of an athlete by teaching him or her new motor skills, it also helps make sure young athletes have a training program that utilizes a principle known as periodization. It is the deliberate introduction of different phases of training – in these phases the program's intensity, frequency, and method of training changes. In a training program without periodization the athlete does the same type of training over and over again year round. If that's done, the returns diminish. In fact, there are negative returns when the same activity is done too often. Instead, what young athletes need is periodic changes in their training schedule. For example, an athlete might play hockey for four months and then participate in a spring sport for two months. By adding in rest, recovery, and training method diversity when training, athletes can maximize their gains and, ultimately, see better results.

Periodization also helps prevent overuse injuries. A multi-sport young athlete is less likely to suffer from overuse injuries than a single sport athlete. Stop Sports Injuries recommends cross training as one method to help prevent injuries. It makes sense, too. By playing multiple sports, the stressors aren't as concentrated and thus the likelihood of overuse injuries decreases. As Dr. Brenner and the Council on Sports Medicine and Fitness wrote, "Young athletes who participate in a variety of sports have fewer injuries and play sports longer than those who specialize before puberty[43]."

Specialize Later to Maximize Gains

Sport specialization isn't necessarily bad for hockey players. In fact, athletes who want to reach the professional and elite levels of their sport will at some point have to specialize. The risk of injury fades after puberty begins. In addition, athletes between around 14 to 17 years old can realize huge gains in speed, agility, and quickness. Unfortunately, if they've been overtraining and overworking in one sport their entire lives, they might miss out on the most important years of training. One Danish study looked at success in sports as measured in centimeters, grams, and seconds (CGS) and concluded, "factors related to the organization of practice during the mid-teens seem to be crucial for international success within cgs sports[44]." Their data shows elite athletes train less than near elite athletes at younger ages, but as they progress through their teenage years, they train quite a bit more.

The following chart shows the accumulated hours over time for these athletes. Notice it was not until about age 18 that the elite players practiced roughly as much as the near elite. Prior to that age, the near elite group actually accumulated more practice hours.

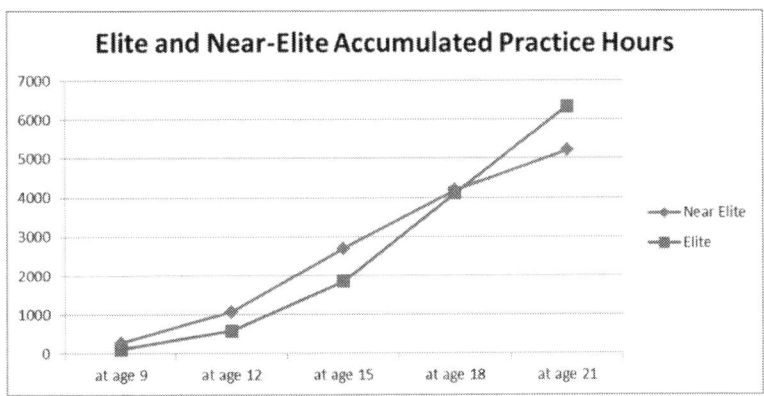

Data Source: Moesch, Karen, A.-M. Elbe, M.-L. T. Hauge, and J. M. Wikman. "Late specialization: the key to success in centimeters, grams, or seconds (cgs) sports."

CGS sports are primarily individual sports that are far less complex and do not involve the same athleticism as team sports. For example, running a 100-meter sprint takes much less (if any) creativity and inventiveness than is required to play hockey. Since CGS sports tend to be more like gymnastics or figure skating in that the sport is pre-planned, it is surprising to find that practicing more at younger ages is not correlated with elite performance later in life.

One interesting data point shows the near elite athletes decreased their weekly training load around ages 12 to 15. The all-important training window, which is discussed further in the training chapter (roughly between ages 14 and 17), is missed. Many of the near elite athletes trained *less* during this period, not more. Why? Perhaps they lost motivation to keep training with such high frequency and intensity, or they might have gotten injured.

The results of this study are not conclusive and I want to make it clear, as so often the proponents of early specialization do not, that this study is correlational. There are many factors that contribute to athletic performance. None-the-less, the correlational data here provides quite a compelling argument against early specialization. In this study, the authors did not find a correlation between the months of involvement in others sports, the number of other sports played, or the elite/near elite status of the players. This does not seem surprising for CGS sports since we might hypothesize that other sports have fewer skills to transfer to CGS sports. For example, sprinting in track helps hockey players more than playing hockey helps a runner. Sprinting increases speed - a key component of athleticism in hockey. It's unclear to me how hockey would significantly increase sprinting performance in track.

Tommy John, the former baseball player for whom the pitcher's surgery is named, agrees athletes don't need to start playing one sport year round when they're young. John believes the following: "I can take a kid who has never pitched in his life until he's seventeen. By the time he's nineteen he'll throw as well as or better than the kid who's been pitching since he was eight – and have less wear and tear on his arm[45]." The only reason John can make a statement like this is when athletes are mid-to-late teens they have an extraordinary ability to improve athletically. The key for an athlete is to practice and train at 100 percent with proper nutrition and direction during these key three to four years.

There are plenty of stories about young hockey players who played on C-level teams during their youth, but eventually played varsity in high school. Sometimes the player no one thought would make it past Bantams ends up playing college hockey. Often times, a player's transformation occurs in the pivotal years following puberty. Since the onset of puberty varies, the biological edge early bloomers once had begins to fade over time. The playing field begins to even out. During these pivotal years for training, it is amazing to the see the gains athletes make in speed, agility, explosiveness, and quickness.

Keep It Fun

As sports have moved from pickup games to organized institutions, a lot of deliberate practice and development has been instituted. The expectation to be the best has caused many parents to equate practice with improvement. Unfortunately, the two don't always correlate positively. Especially at young ages (under 13 years old), it is important for young athletes to have fun and to play. There is a reason hockey is called a "game" and not a "job."

During the regular hockey season, the importance placed on games and the need to "win" harms the development of many youngsters. In youth hockey programs there should be more creative, free play drills and small games instead of the monotonous drill after drill repetition model advocated by many. Drills are important and help build certain skills, but many coaches overemphasize them. Free play and small games help athletes build creativity and reaction skills that few, if any, drills can do as effectively.

If there were a frozen pond available year round that hockey players could play on whenever they wished – every single day, if they chose – it would not harm them at all. Yet, if put under the direction of a coach and "forced" to do drill after drill, the fun only lasts so long.

Research has shown that those athletes who begin specialized training earlier tend to dropout and burnout more than those who wait. For example, in a study published by Wall and Cote (2007) they discovered "ice hockey players who dropped out of the sport had begun off-ice training earlier than athletes who continued their participation[46]." The study did not sample a large number of players but the findings make sense. Off-ice training is arguably far less enjoyable – especially specialized off-ice training – than playing on the rink. Perhaps the most convincing argument, however, for keeping the game fun at the youngest levels are the results of a retrospective study conducted by Cote and Soberlak. They quantified the number of hours spent per year doing four different types of practice for 20-year-old professional hockey players: deliberate practice, deliberate play, organized games, and other sports. The chart below shows the results.

Deliberate Practice and Deliberate Play

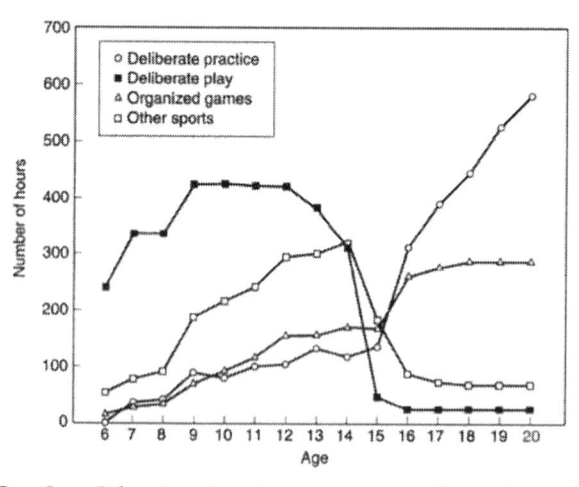

Source: Cote, Jean, Baker, Joseph and Bruce Abernethy. "From Play to Practice: A Developmental Framework for the Acquisition of Expertise in Team Sports."

Before age 15, these professional hockey players spent more hours per year doing deliberate play than deliberate practice[47]. They also played other sports more than they deliberately practiced for hockey. Looking at the total accumulated hours for each type of training is even more illuminating:

Total Hours Spent on Deliberate Play/Practice, Organized Games, and Other Sports

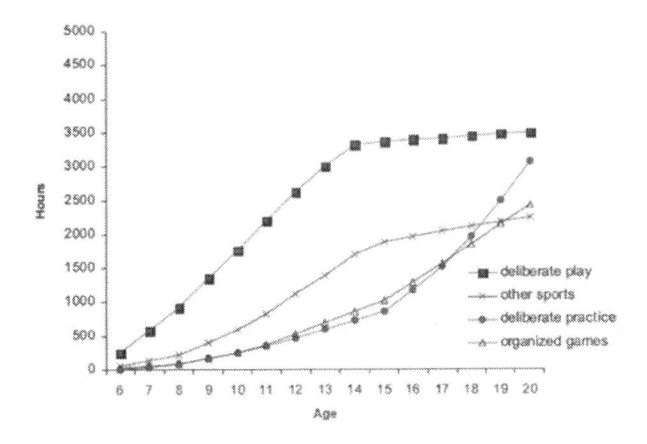

Source: Soberlak, Peter, and Jean Cote. "The Developmental Activities of Elite Ice Hockey Players."

    To maximize skill development, players need a wide array of drills, intermixing specific skills with creative free play drills. Sports like hockey, football, basketball, lacrosse and soccer require creative thinking, not just the ability to repeat movements in structured environments over and over again. One example of this difference is found in two passing drills. Partner passing drills have two players pass the puck with each other. This is a simple drill that works on a specific skill.

Another passing drill is called "Monkey in the Middle". In this game, one player stands in the middle of the circle while the rest of the players (four to six) stand on the edges. The outside players have to keep the puck away from the player in the middle by passing it as fast as possible to different players around the circle. This game forces players to pass like partner passing, but it adds unknown variables to the mix. Players must keep their heads up, communicate, and anticipate the movements of the player inside the circle. A game like this will draw more attention and focus from the players than a rote partner pass drill.

The 10,000 Hour Rule: Fact or Fiction?

One common theory often cited as evidence for the need to specialize early is the 10,000 Hour Rule. The rule states an individual needs to perform at least 10,000 hours of practice to become elite in any domain. Two researchers, Simon and Chase, first presented the concept in 1973. They came to this conclusion after discovering that chess players "must have played chess for at least ten years before they are able to win international chess tournaments[48]." The 10,000 Hour Rule has become popularized more recently by Malcom Gladwell's book *Outliers* where he cites research conducted by K. Anders Ericsson. At Berlin's Academy of Music Ericsson discovered the difference between violin students considered elite, good and not likely to play professionally was the amount of accumulated practice hours. In Gladwell's words, "by the age of twenty, the elite performers had each totaled ten thousand hours of practice. By contrast, the merely good students had totaled eight thousand hours[49]." The least skilled group "had totaled just over four thousand hours[50]."

Gladwell goes on to assert that "without ten thousand hours" of practice, no hockey player or participant in any activity can possibly "master the skills necessary to play at the top level[51]." If 10,000 hours is required for elite performance, the argument made is young athletes should start accumulating hours so they become elite players. Unfortunately, obtaining expert performance in hockey and any other activity is not so simple.

First of all, Ericsson argues that elite performance can't be obtained simply through experience – it requires deliberate practice that is designed to increase a person's abilities. Second, Ericsson points out there are instances when the 10,000 hour rule doesn't hold. He writes that extremely tall basketball players have entered the professional ranks in around six years and "research on training of memory experts has shown that individuals can reach the highest level in the world after less than a couple years of training[52]." Professor Cote at the University of Ontario argues, "expert performance in sports has been achieved with 3,000 to 4,000 hours of sport specific training[53]." (The athlete will have practiced more than 3,000 to 4,000 hours if we include unstructured practice and play). Jason Gulbin Ph.D. from the National Talent Search Program with the Australian Institute of Sport writes in a symposium given in Berlin, "for a large proportion of the Australian high performance sport system, the 10-year development 'rule of thumb' does not apply, and furthermore, accelerated development can occur with late specialization[54]."

Another reason why elite performance may be achieved prior to 10 years or 10,000 hours of deliberate practice is because training gains vary dramatically depending on the age of the athlete. For example, aerobic training in young children can produce a positive training response, but the response "will be only about 50% of that expected in young adults[55]." In addition, the "exercise intensities for pre-pubertal children must be higher than those for young adults – requiring heart rates of 170-180 beats per minute…for training adaptions to be realized[56]." In other words, a young adult can achieve the aerobic gains obtained from a youth athlete training 1,000 hours in roughly half the time and by exerting less energy. Gains in strength and muscle mass are also highly dependent on the physical preparedness of the athlete. It is possible to increase strength through resistance training, for example, prior to puberty. However, the strength increases come primarily from neural adaptations, not muscle mass growth.

Perhaps the difference between Ericsson's research on violinists and the studies regarding athletes put forth here is the type of learning required to master either domain. Learning to play chess or the violin is far different than learning to play a sport. In the first two instances, the primary requirement is to obtain the necessary intellectual capacity. Sports do require mental effort, but the physical requirements are much higher. Consider the chart on the following page.

NORMAL GROWTH PATTERNS

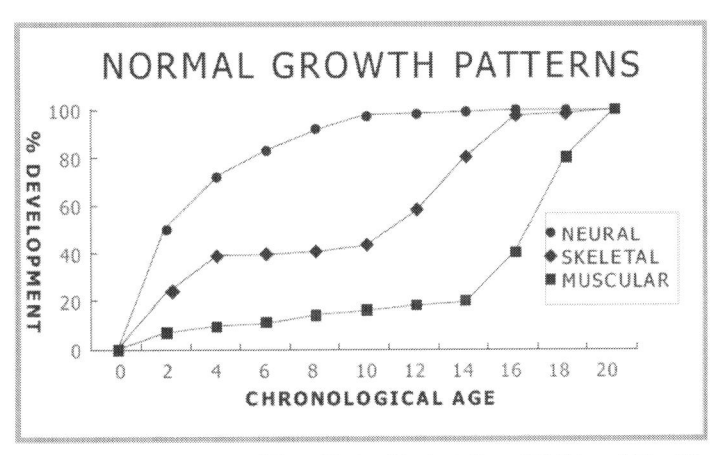

Chart showing % Development vs Chronological Age (0-20), with three curves: Neural, Skeletal, and Muscular.

Source: Anderson, Gregory, and Peter Twist. "Trainability of Children." Idea Fitness.

Notice how neural growth patterns peak around age 10 with a significant majority of neural development occurring by age eight. Interestingly, the violinists in Ericsson's study practiced roughly the same amount of time until age eight when roughly 90 percent of neurological growth has occurred. At this point, Gladwell points out "students who would end up the best in their class began to practice more than everyone else[57]."

In the Danish study on elite athletes in CGS sports, the elite athletes did not accumulate more hours of practice until age 18, but they practiced more on a weekly basis around age 15. Prior to that age, the body still has about 80 percent of normal growth to achieve. Between the ages of 15 and 20, the majority of muscular growth occurs. During this time, hormonal changes allow athletes to achieve massive gains in speed and quickness and eventually size and strength. One hypothesis is violinists who practice at younger ages return significant gains in skill whereas athletes with training gains in certain areas (like strength and size) are limited by physiological factors.

The other issue with applying the 10,000 Hour Rule too early is it is predicated upon deliberate practice. Ericsson writes that this type of practice requires "full attention and concentration[58]" and the correction of errors that arise during practice. Deliberate practice is not necessarily fun. It requires an ability to persist at a given task that can often be mundane, for extended periods of time. Young athletes want to play and have fun. They want to be creative. The intensity of young athletes' efforts decreases significantly and their concentration wanes when they are asked to perform drills for too long. Practice doesn't make perfect; it makes for permanent. The positive effects of practice are most likely negated when athletes are no longer concentrating, enjoying themselves, and putting forth a good effort.

Early Identification Programs Don't Work

Early identification programs focus on early specialization. These programs supposedly pick the "best" young hockey players, as young as six years old, and train them. They say the best talent needs to be identified and trained early. If this method is used, its proponents argue, better talent can be developed.

There are several problems with early identification programs. The most obvious is they don't identify the best talent very well. Conclusive studies show elite players have not always been considered elite. In fact, "researchers have previously reported that exceptional success and performance by juvenile athletes appeared to be neither a necessary nor a sufficient prerequisite for later success[59]." Researchers discovered in 2009 that early identification programs of German Olympians actually correlated negatively with long term success:

> *"Early participation in competitions and inclusion in talent identification and talent promotion programs correlated negatively with long term senior success. Only the training volume in other sports (beyond the current main sport) displayed significant differentiating effects on later success in senior elite sport[60]."*

Jean Cote and Bruce Abernethy in a chapter titled "A Developmental Approach to Sport Expertise" in The Oxford Handbook of Sport and Performance Psychology, state that early identification programs don't work. They write that the "long term prediction of talent in athletes is unreliable, especially talent detection attempted during the pre-pubertal and pubertal periods[61]". One of Cote's studies looked at Portuguese male and female athletes in four sports: soccer, volleyball, swimming, and judo. They looked at how many athletes selected to play on the pre-junior international team went on to play for the junior and senior international teams. They discovered "only around a third of…early selected athletes reappeared among top athletes at the senior level[62]." The early selected athletes were males 16 years old or younger in all four sports. In soccer, swimming, and judo only 34.1, 30, and 28.1 percent, respectively, of the pre-junior team members competed at the senior level. In other words, only one third of these top 16-year-old athletes in these sports continued playing at the elite level beyond age 19.

Contrast this research with the hockey model being promoted by AAA programs. This model contends that a lack of competition and "the wide gap in ability between the top and bottom players on the same team" hurts the development of the best players[63]. The differentiating between players starts at a very young age, as young as mites who are seven or eight years old. Parents striving to do what is best for their children often fall prey to the enticing logic that their son or daughter is elite, unique, and special. They are thus told it is necessary to fork over additional money, time, and resources to pursue truly elite training. If they don't do this, they'll risk their player's hockey future.

Judging hockey players at such an early age by identifying the "talented" ones inhibits the future development of many other hockey players. At these young ages, it's not possible to identify which players will become the best in future years. Physically the players will grow at rapid, but disproportionate rates. Some will grow quickly and then slow down while others do the opposite. Instead of shrinking the pool of players that receive quality training, every single player should be given a chance to become the best he or she can.

Early identification programs provide "an early advantage to a selected number of children who are often chosen because of their accelerated maturity[64]." Malcom Gladwell, in his book *Outliers*, explains that players who are born soon after the arbitrary cut off dates for playing levels disproportionately become the elite players.

> *"An iron law of Canadian hockey: in any elite group of hockey players – the very best of the best – 40 percent of the players will have been born between January and March, 30 percent between April and June, 20 percent between July and September, and 10 percent between October and December[65]."*

How is this occurring? When players are six or seven years old, the difference between someone born in January and November is large. Developmentally, two athletes, one born in January and the other in November should be considered different ages when playing sports because their physical maturity differs so greatly. Yet, we don't do this, and the oldest players at any given level have quite an advantage over everyone else. They are put on the best teams that generally have the best coaching so they improve far more quickly than those who are not provided these same opportunities.

In fact, one parent once told me the association his athlete played for "only plans for the A-team[66]." This puts a lot of pressure on the athlete to "make the A-team because the alternative may mean poor coaching and a long season with no real improvement[67]." The statistics, if players born in the months between October and December in Canada were given the proper skill development opportunities, there would be more competition to make it into the elite ranks.

The Truth about College and Professional Hockey

What makes the argument for specialization even more absurd (beyond the fact that it doesn't help athletes become better athletes, or that those who promote it obviously have interests that may conflict with those they are training) are the statistics. Even if we assume that specialization in team sports is necessary to create amazing athletes, we must deal with the reality that only a small percentage of athletes can truly be elite athletes. Few players will play college athletics at the Division I level and even fewer will make it to the professional ranks.

The likelihood that a youth hockey player will play college athletics at the Division I (DI) or Division III (DIII) level is extremely small. Of those male hockey players that make it to the high school varsity level, the NCAA estimates that 10.8 percent will play men's ice hockey at a NCAA member institution[68]. This statistic includes DI and DIII schools. Tom Keegan, the editor of multiple hockey guides, concluded based on 2006/7 data that "8.57% of prep and private school players continue playing hockey at the NCAA level" whereas less than 1% of public school players move on to the next level[69].

Parents often think if their students make it to the collegiate level it is a huge plus because they'll receive college scholarships. Often this isn't true. The NCAA limits the amount of scholarships awarded to any given DI team to 18. There were 27 hockey players listed on the 2011-12 University of Minnesota hockey team. Coaches can split scholarships so more players receive them, but ultimately there isn't a guarantee money will be available. Some colleges don't offer the total amount of scholarships they are allowed, and the Ivy League does not offer any at all.

Parents should also question the value of the education itself, even if their son or daughter does end up getting a college hockey scholarship. Recent research conducted by William G. Bowen, former President of Princeton University, demonstrates that athletes are actually *underperforming* in college at our Ivy League and highly selective Division III colleges. That is, given how well they did in high school, they do worse than we'd expect in college. Bowen found:

> *"While the SAT scores of football, basketball, and hockey players in the Ivy League rose by over 60 points between 1976 and 1989, and while the SATs of students at large at these schools rose by only 38 points, the mean rank-in-class of Ivy League High Profile athletes continued to fall, and an ever larger share of them ended up in the bottom third of the class[70]."*

Bowen found this underperformance also to be true at Division III coed liberal arts colleges where "statistically significant degrees of underperformance are observed on a consistent basis[71]."

There are several plausible explanations for athlete's underperformance. There is speculation that the time requirements in athletics essentially distracts from academic achievement and that underperformance can be explained by a lack of time for studies. Bowen investigated this hypothesis by comparing athletic participation with student activities that required a similar level of commitment. He found students in these other extracurricular activities over performed relative to expectations. The students in these other extracurricular activities "were editors of the student newspaper, presidents of student government, or involved in orchestra or the theater at a similar level of commitment[72]." All of those activities require substantial time commitments and make it difficult for those participating in them to devote time to strictly academic work. Yet, Bowen found they overachieved relative to expectations.

In addition, Bowen analyzed football player grades in season during the fall semester and out-of-season in the spring semester. What he found was "recruited football players who played in the sophomore year underperformed by 24 points in the fall and 20 points in the spring[73]." That is, the player's percentile rank-in-class was 24 points lower in the fall and 20 points lower in the spring than would be expected given their academic history. The data likely shows time constraints are not the primary cause of underperformance, but rather other variable or variables.

Underperformance is not the only issue academically. Student-athletes in college tend to cluster into the easiest social science or humanities majors. Take for instance Steven Cline, a football player at Kansas State University. He entered college wanting to become a veterinarian. He ended up graduating with a degree in social sciences and working at a construction site in order to save up enough money to go back to school. Cline felt he had "just wasted" all his hard work and "efforts in high school and college to get a social science degree[74]." In order to stay eligible and focus on football, Cline was advised to switch to an easier major – one which "drew 34% of the football team's juniors and seniors…compared with 4% of all juniors and seniors at Kansas State[75]."

The only well-paying job a hockey player will receive with a similar education after graduation is in the NHL. Yet, the likelihood of making it to the NHL, even for those young athletes who made it to the high school hockey ranks, is low. Only .1 percent of *these high school hockey players* will go on to play in the professional ranks[76]. The percentage chance a high school athlete in men's basketball, women's basketball, football, baseball, men's ice hockey, and men's soccer will make it to a NCAA member institution is 3.2, 3.6, 6.1, 6.6, 10.7, and 5.7 percent, respectively[77]. The likelihood these high school athletes will make it to the professional ranks, according to NCAA Research, is less than 1 percent and as seen in the table below:

Percentage of Players from High School to Professional Ranks

Women's Basketball	Men's Basketball	Baseball	Men's Ice Hockey	Football	Men's Soccer
.03%	.03%	.60%	.10%	.08%	.04%

The statistics don't get much brighter for college athletes. Ken Campbell, in an article on ESPN.com wrote in 2007, "in college hockey, Hockey East led the way with 11 NHLers among 162 players for 6.8 percent. The WCHA was next at nine among 162 for a 5.6 percent showing. The CCHA had six NHLers among 198 players for 3.0 percent and the ECAC had eight among 216 for 3.7 percent[78]." Even if an athlete plays in college, a wonderful accomplishment, the chances are quite small hockey will provide him or her a living. For athletes who don't make it to the NHL, their value in the job market will be very much determined by the quality of education they've received. Sure, hockey can, and does, instill certain values like hard work and teamwork that are positive workforce attributes, but these values don't offset serious academic neglect.

Another reason to know the statistics is athletes often are misled into thinking their chances of success are far greater than they truly are, and therefore become discouraged from working hard in school or in other areas of their lives. Especially when the emphasis from parents and coaches is so intense to become a better athlete and little attention is paid to academic success. Young athletes are very perceptive to the system of reward our culture and society presents them. Seeing the extent to which strong athletes receive attention, it should come to no one's surprise that young athletes might de-emphasize school work in order to achieve more athletically.

The associated opportunity costs with the relentless training and focus on playing high school varsity, college, and professional hockey are enormous. The financial burden alone prohibits many athletes from playing hockey, especially in areas where the best coaching and competition requires a large down payment. Hockey is so expensive, in fact, that if parents were to invest the money they spent on hockey in a college savings fund, I think many families would have accumulated enough money to provide their children with scholarships.

Unfortunately, money is not the only opportunity cost. Hockey requires a lot of time. For every hour a young athlete plays hockey, it necessarily subtracts one hour from some other activity (family, study time, and other extracurricular activities). There are many advantages to playing sport, like reduced risk of obesity, but the benefits of sport at some point provide diminished returns and can even create a slew of negative consequences. Young athletes lose out on study time, and even if they perform at a high level academically, they might be achieving less than their potential. Considering how competitive hockey families I know are, I find it surprising that more are not alarmed and angry that American children are lagging in math and science relative to their international peers. The health benefits of sports might also turn negative, especially if overuse injuries occur. We don't know yet what all the long term healthcare consequences of these injuries are, but even in the short term, they are negative.

Before concluding this chapter, I want to emphasize that despite the statistics, I believe all youth athletes should be allowed and encouraged to pursue their dreams of playing sports, regardless of their perceived potential. At times, those who have advocated for late specialization and a reduced emphasis on early specialized training have been stereotyped as uncompetitive. Some see these advocates as not caring enough whether or not their athletes join the college or professional ranks. Let me be clear where I stand. As a hockey trainer and extremely competitive person, I design training programs with the goal of the athlete realizing the very best developmental gains. I believe early specialization is not only bad for the health of young athletes, but *also* destructive to their athletic development. I would like to see hockey training programs become more innovative and forward thinking so more players compete for spots on elite teams.

How to Stop Early Specialization and Promote Community Based Hockey

How do we stop early specialization in hockey and other sports? Let's take the case of Minnesota hockey. AAA organizations and hockey training facilities have ballooned across the state. The same has been true throughout the country in many different sports. These new organizations are being added to or replacing the current community hockey system. For those not familiar with the "old" system of hockey because they live on the East Coast or elsewhere in the country, consider how hockey is played in Minnesota. It is an extremely popular sport. Almost every community has a hockey program. Children grow up skating with their friends, dreaming of making the high school hockey team, and playing in the state high school championship. Community-based hockey is relatively inexpensive, and is far more affordable than AAA programs offered elsewhere in the country.

In other parts of the country, competitive hockey leagues and decent training programs only can be found by joining a AAA organization. In Minnesota, community-based hockey leagues cost anywhere from a few hundred dollars to nearly $2,000 per season. The price tag is much higher elsewhere. As John Russo writes in a Let's Play Hockey article, "in most states, there are organizations like Team Illinois, Chicago Young Americans, Belle Tire…and so on that cost $15,000 to $20,000 to play for[79]." The costs of these programs effectively limit the sport to only the wealthiest of families. If the pool of players and the amount of talent available is shrunk, then the state of hockey throughout the country is hurt.

Community-hockey on the East Coast is almost nonexistent. In Minnesota, the trend today is toward greater specialization in hockey and more AAA programs that offer year round training. These programs cost a lot of money and although not as outrageous as the organizations mentioned previously, they are, in effect, pricing out families in a sport that is inherently already expensive. Not only that, but AAA programs are businesses and they need to protect their brand. If a AAA program doesn't win games, players don't sign up to tryout, and the money isn't there. The net affect can be turning away players who can't make the cut. This happens at early ages, too. For instance, one AAA program claims that association hockey is "rarely a good fit for the passionate Mite families, elite or potential elite players[80]." Why is that? Many reasons, but one reason I mentioned earlier is the "wide gap in ability between the top and bottom players on the same team[81]" in the traditional community associations. The problem is talent identification programs do not work! A disproportionate amount of older players in each level will be identified as being more elite or potentially elite. Furthermore, those players who mature slower than others will be unfairly shut out of hockey simply because their biological growth level is different than their peers. The expensive leagues have the best coaching and skill development. As a result, those unable to afford these leagues are stuck in less competitive and generally less well-coached teams. Over time, the quality of competition and skill development in the community programs is diminished. The only way to play competitively becomes to pay far more than the average American family can afford. As more families drop out of the sport, it becomes more expensive.

In Minnesota, community organizations have tried to fight back against the rising tide of AAA programs. In fact, District 6, one of the local governing boards for the community associations, made a rule that no player could play in the Minnesota Made Choice League and in the association at the same time. Minnesota Made took them to court over the ruling. The issue was resolved outside of court, but the details were not disclosed to the public.

The problem with this approach is we live in a free country and trying to force players to stay in the community programs through the court system will never work. Youth sports parents and their players make judgments about where to play and how much to play based on the information they have. Parents are being misled in many ways. The market has a high level of information asymmetry – the entrepreneur knows a lot, the parent knows very little, and this creates a situation conducive to bad decision making. Parents don't understand that talent identification is a bad policy and one that results is less development over the long term.

The solution is simple: community organizations need to inform parents, educate them, and offer competitive clinics, camps, and programs. Youth sports organizations are community led but they often lack the desire or will to market themselves like a business. However, that is what really successful programs do. They inform, engage and sell their service or product to parents. Youth organizations need to do this to survive. They can't implicitly raise the white flag of surrender to the preachers of the early specialization gospel. They also must realize that to combat the forces of early specialization and high intensity training, they need to compare their services to those who fail to adhere to the science of hockey training.

Organizations and private companies that do not work in the best interests of hockey players need to be identified by community associations. This is what private pay-to-play leagues have done to gain business. They declare the community organizations just don't get it. They don't know how to train. After all, dads lead many of these organizations, some of who have never even played the sport they coach. It's all fair game. Community programs need to understand they are competing and if they don't do so aggressively, and soon, they will be diminished to the status of uncompetitive recreational leagues.

Community associations also should partner with hockey training companies to help provide top notch training. Business can be an important part of the solution to the problem. Youth associations should adapt and allow for those who have time and incentive to become a part of their programs. If youth associations attempt to keep everything in-house and push out entrepreneurs and innovative thinkers, they will lose. The innovators not only have an incentive to introduce new ideas, they also have the incentive to sell their services. Community organizations often depend upon volunteers who have far fewer incentives.

To reap the benefits of for profit companies without becoming them, community associations can merge the two models together. They should look to reap the benefits of incentivizing development and progress while simultaneously providing the community framework needed for long term player growth. For example, a Mite clinic for a local association might be structured to include a well-paid, knowledgeable coach leading the session with five to seven parents volunteering as assistant coaches. In this example, the local association may provide quality training, similar to that provided elsewhere, for a much more affordable price. This allows the community association to increase its numbers – the more Mite hockey players, the bigger the talent pool, and the more potential an association has to develop great hockey players.

Community programs also can offer training methods that can't be sold at high prices. For example, one of the best ways to develop a passion for hockey and the creativity needed for success is to play the game in a fun, adult free environment. Community associations can, for a much lower cost, put together training programs that include large amounts of pond hockey, especially at the younger ages. Imagine running a 3v3 pond hockey session on an Olympic size rink for Squirts. The rink can be split into thirds. In each section of the rink two teams can scrimmage and each team can be comprised of roughly 10 players. Sixty players can fit onto one sheet of ice! Ice in Minnesota costs around $200 a sheet or less. Even at the high end, the per player cost is just over $3 per time. For young families, this is cheaper than day care.

Off-Ice Training

Chapter 2

Introduction

Athleticism is not easy to define because for each sport it requires a different mix of physical attributes and mental capabilities. Regardless of its sport specific composition, it is a complex equation that includes a long list of variables. Yet many athletic training programs tend to be rather singular in their focus. They neglect the complexities of athleticism for a cleaner, easier one size fits all approach. These programs seem rigid, with little variation between workouts, let alone over significant time periods. The football players and hockey players do the same workouts since in these programs football athleticism is essentially comparable to hockey athleticism. These programs are unimaginative and do not maximize sport specific gains.

I entered the training world when I met Jack Blatherwick. He trained the 1980 U.S. Olympic Team and I feel blessed to have met him. Blatherwick didn't accept the common training philosophies, and I liked that about him. He was always thinking and striving to better understand how to help athletes develop *athleticism*. Since meeting Blatherwick I have taken a similar "outside-the-box" approach to training.

I'll explain the general framework we use with Fortis to approach athletic training. When we first trained a cheerleading team, we did a thorough examination of the sport to understand the athleticism required to be successful in it. At the time, my partner, Jake Villas, and I didn't know anything about cheerleading. But we analyzed the sport and asked for help from the coaches. What movements do the cheerleaders perform? Where does having added strength help a cheerleader perform better? How long are competitions? What type of endurance is needed? What are the mental obstacles? We asked more questions until we understood every physical movement of the sport. We didn't focus on the strategic or tactical aspects; we knew what muscles were used, and what type of athleticism was needed (mentally and physically).

After understanding the sport, we didn't twist the physical requirements of the sport to match our existing training programs. We created new training programs to match the sport. Over time, we experimented. We incorporated balance drills for the flyers (the athletes who are held in the air, stand on one foot, etc.) Our base players, the girls that hold the flyers in the air, did a lot plyometric training that resembled a hockey workout. The stronger their legs, the easier they could lift and control the flyers. The intent was to get the cheerleaders to the point where they could swiftly squat and raise the flyer into position. We never thought we knew it all. Throughout the summer training program, we brainstormed and tried new and innovative ways to train the cheerleaders.

Many programs mold the game to fit the training programs they've created. In this chapter I will discuss how hockey athletes should train. Knowing when to do a certain type of training is just as important as knowing what kind of training to do. And, as athletes train, I want them to ask themselves: "How will this help make me become a better hockey player?" How does this training program help build the type of athleticism I need to be successful?

Weight Training: The myth, the legend, and the truth

One of the greatest tragedies and unfortunate aspects to youth sports training is the mindsets many youth hockey players, parents, and coaches have toward weight training. Specifically, the role weight training should have in a hockey player's training program is often severely overstated, misplaced, or misunderstood. The problem originates from student high school psychology. When hockey players enter the high school weight room for the first time in their freshman year or just prior, they see the older high school athletes. Most of the young athletes look up to these players and want to emulate them. They see the high school linebacker's chest and biceps or senior varsity hockey captain's bench press and want to emulate these players. They want to get bigger and stronger, too. Since older athletes are lifting very heavy weights, it seems logical to the mind of a fourteen- year-old that he or she should lift very heavy weights too. Often the consequences of this desire are sacrificed technique, higher risk of injury, and almost zero athletic benefits.

Unfortunately, high school coaches and trainers sometimes don't help. I have seen "certified" trainers give scrawny and pre-pubescent boys the same workouts as the 18-year-old young men who have hair on their chest. This is one of the most dangerous and absurd aspects to athletic training today. It is absolutely wrong that 14-year-old boys are doing the same type of training as 17 or 18-year-olds. Most 14-year-old boys are not ready to bulk up. In fact, Mayo Clinic states that bulking up is "most safely done after adolescence[82]." Fortunately, this problem is not currently as prevalent among females.

Coaches contribute to the problem by simply emphasizing the importance of getting into the weight room. They'll tell their players: "you better hit the weights if you want to play varsity some day!" Sure, weight training is necessary, but shouldn't we differentiate between the youngest and oldest players? When working with hockey teams or groups that span a variety of ages, trainers should make clear to the very youngest that their goals aren't so much mass gains but rather speed/quickness improvements. The older players can do weight training to build mass but the younger players should not waste time trying to achieve this goal. Maximum return on investment for young players comes from speed, quickness, and agility training.

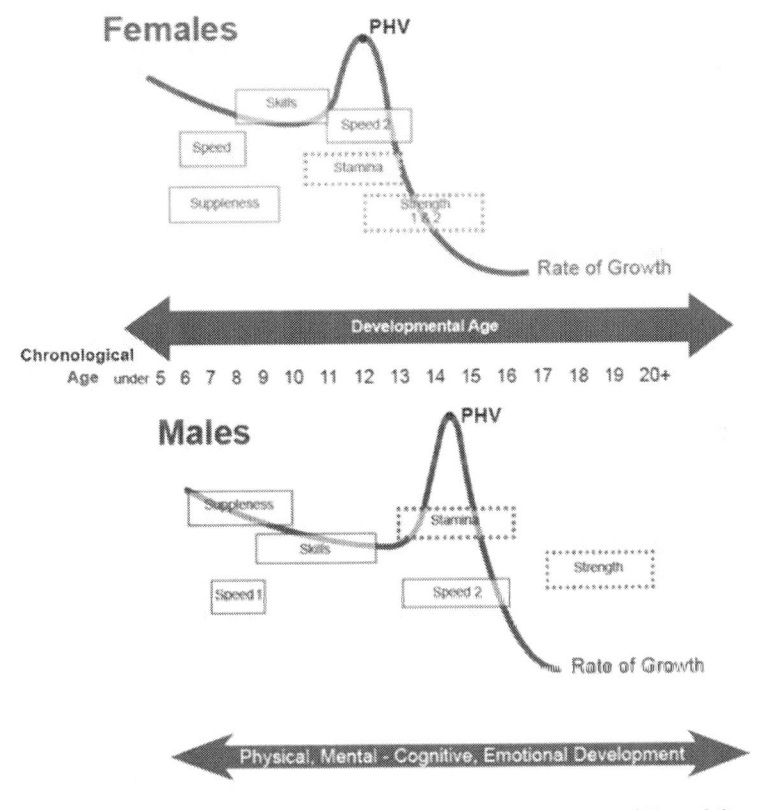

Source: USAHOCKEY Development Model, Windows of Trainability
http://wwa.usahockey.com/ADMKids_Coaches.aspx

It is imperative to differentiate between the maturation levels of athletes when training. First off, the physical development of strength, as shown by the chart from USA Hockey, occurs when an athlete is 17 years old or older. Readers should note that female development occurs a couple years earlier than male development in the chart.

During these key years, an athlete can lift weights, gain mass quickly, and increase strength. Young male athletes can make amazing transformations during this period. Fourteen-year-olds have not gone through puberty and do not have the necessary testosterone levels to build mass. Instead of being able to build muscle, athletes at this critical age are able to do something they'll never be able to do again (to the same extent) for the rest of their lives – build speed. When athletes are 14 or 15 years old and until puberty really sets in, they have an amazing ability to get quicker and faster with the proper training. The problem is often times that these fruitful years for athletic gains are sacrificed by mindless weight lifting.

The problem is many trainers and coaches tend to equate size with athletic ability. It's an odd concept. Take for instance the equation Force = Mass * Acceleration. To increase force, an athlete does not need to increase mass; he or she can increase acceleration. Now, if an athlete increases mass, what is the likelihood the athlete will *decrease* acceleration? At some point in hockey, size becomes detrimental because the benefits gained are eclipsed by its disadvantages (the primary one being a reduction in speed). Increase acceleration, but do not need decrease mass. Athletes can sprint and maintain weight whereas it is harder to gain weight and maintain sprinting speeds.

Resistance training can be used with athletes as young as seven years old and strength gains can be made, according to Mayo Clinic[83]. However, mass gains – besides those that naturally accompany growth – cannot be achieved. The reason young athletes get stronger is because "the nervous system is highly trainable at a young age[84]." When learning a new motor skill like skating, different lifts can be more quickly learned. Young athletes that weight train, however, need to be closely supervised by a professional and shouldn't lift heavy weights or do lifts where muscles are exhausted. There are serious risks with doing so.

Weight lifting and strength training should be taught to young athletes as a standard practice by the ages of 14 to 16 and used more aggressively thereafter in order to gain mass. To attempt to gain mass before a male athlete has the necessary testosterone levels is a waste of time and potentially harmful. Most freshman boys are not ready and should not indulge in lots of weight lifting.

What they should be doing is sprinting – a lot. They should be sprinting as much as possible to increase their speed. In addition, they should be working on agility and footwork. These are all skills they are ready to develop. Unfortunately, in a few years the gains they will get from these types of training will be diminished. No more substantial gains in speed, and agility drills may start to get more difficult as they pack more muscle and mass onto their frames. Even as players get older, the emphasis tends to be lopsided. Plyometric training, agility work, and sprints are essential to athleticism.

Elite athletes have explosiveness, agility, quickness, and speed. If an athlete has these attributes, but does not have strength, NHL scouts know through proper training they can get stronger, even at older ages. However, a scout watching a slow but really strong player will not have the same response. How likely is it that this athlete will increase his or her speed enough? Not likely. Athletes can always get stronger as they mature into young adulthood, but they will not always be able to get faster. That is something every young 14-year-old hockey player must understand.

I'm not saying young athletes shouldn't weight train. They should be training, but the methods should be different. The weight lifting and strength training young athletes do should be geared toward teaching them proper technique and form. Often young athletes want to impress their peers or the varsity coach. They put a lot of weight on the squat rack and improperly exercise. The weight is too heavy for them to do the exercise correctly so they cheat just a little. Then they add more weight and before you know it, the athlete isn't even doing something that resembles a squat. Young athletes will add too much weight and strain their backs or push their knees forward over their toes. This can cause knee and back issues and must be avoided. Now, this tendency to put too much weight on for a given exercise inevitably leads to bad form in a multitude of exercises.

The second unfortunate consequence – besides not really benefiting much in terms of muscle gains, and often not much in strength gains – is when a young athlete matures enough and is ready for mass gains, he or she does not know how to lift properly! Athletes will benefit a lot when it comes to gain mass from being taught proper weight training technique. They will get slightly stronger, but more importantly they'll learn the movements. Exercises like the squat are not intuitive and take time to master correctly. It also takes a very committed and engaged trainer. Generally, working with 18-year-olds is easy because they should know how to do the lifts. Younger, inexperienced athletes take a lot more work and constant correction until they master each lift. Athletes' bodies will gain mass very quickly once they mature and have used proper form and technique.

Hockey players need to get away from archaic forms of training that stress size over strength. Size and strength are not always the same thing, and weight training at the neglect of more explosive and athletic training would be unwise. There is a proper place for weight training as long as it's not overused. If I were to ask any athlete which is harder: bench press and bicep curls or explosive sprints and plyometric training, I think most would say the latter is. It's not only physically more tiring, but it's also extremely mentally taxing.

Weight training should be considered a secondary training method for hockey players. And when hockey players do utilize weight training, a variety of different methodologies can and should be used. There is a place for the stationary strength movements, but athletes should also do movements that are more dynamic and relatable to hockey.

There are several different goals for weight training. It can be used for strength training. Strength is defined as the ability to exert force on mass so as to move it – the speed and quickness of this movement is irrelevant. The only goal is to lift the weight. Muscular endurance is achieved through weight training as well. Muscular endurance is the ability to do a repetitive movement for an extended period of time. Explosiveness and power gains also can be realized in the weight room. Explosiveness is the ability to lift weight quickly. On the bench press, it means being able to extend the bar from the lowest position near the sternum to the starting position with arms reaching out as far as possible.

Still, the gains an athlete can achieve from weight training in terms of strength, muscular endurance, power, and explosiveness need to be understood within the context of the game. A bench press is a good exercise, but does it really help train hockey specific *athleticism*? Everything a hockey player does to train *for* hockey should be understood within the context of the sport. This isn't to say that cross training should be neglected. In fact, hockey players should include cross training and play other sports that have little relation to hockey (at least outwardly). This helps players build different motor skills, learn a new game, or utilize their muscles in a different way.

Utilizing Weight Training to Build Muscle Mass

Let's now focus on the different types of weight training a hockey player can do and how each of these types of training relate to the game. I give little direction here in exact training regiments. Instead my aim is to give a blueprint or guide to training that can be used in all contexts to help a hockey player and family understand what training is important and what to avoid.

Gaining size tends to be the most obvious result of weight training and the most praised. Yet, before addressing how to gain mass by utilizing weight training, it is important to ask the most fundamental question: "How does it relate to hockey?" On the one hand, size is a valuable asset in hockey. It is a rough game. If you've ever watched NHL guys battle it out in the corner, you've seen just how physical the game can get. At the same time, hockey is different from sports like basketball or football. The puck is on the ice (ground), and not in the air. Being tall in basketball has its obvious advantages, and at certain positions in football, it does too. But in hockey, size isn't everything. There are two reasons. First, when athletes get too big, they start to slow down. There's a reason it's so hard for huge hockey players to skate fast. They're carrying a lot of weight around. Second, strength in hockey comes from the legs in a squatting position. Anyone standing straight up will be knocked over – you have to be able to skate low. A shorter and more compact athlete will be hard to knock off the puck and so can play the sport alongside much taller players. In the end, size helps, but it has its limitations in the sport of hockey.

Size is also often misconstrued to equal strength. Now, there are different types of strength. There is the ability to simply move the bench press bar up and down and there is the ability to utilize one's legs, oblique muscles, and shoulders to deliver a crushing hit along the boards. It's important not to confuse these types of strength. I prefer to define the latter type of strength as *functional strength* since it applies directly to how strength is utilized in the context of hockey. Still, size isn't the direct equivalent of strength. Even in terms of basic strength. A football player that neglects every lift in the weight room besides the bench press and bicep curls might have a lot to show in outward appearance, but very little once he actually puts the weight on the bar. The human body cannot be compartmentalized in terms of athletic training; the bench press doesn't just require the chest, it also requires good triceps, a strong core, stable back, etc. When working together and synergistically, the body can achieve greater output than it otherwise would be able.

Hockey players should assess their strengths and weaknesses when looking into mass gains. For example, a tall defenseman will benefit more from mass gains than a small agile forward. The smaller forward will never compete with the tall defenseman in terms of mass. At the same time, the tall defenseman will have a hard time being as agile and quick as the small forward. Each should work on their weaknesses, but play to their strengths. Once a player has developed significant muscle gains, the athlete should focus on strength, explosiveness, and power in the weight room. Workouts at this point designed to build mass should be avoided. When male athletes reach the stage where rapid muscle mass occurs, they should look to build the necessary mass and simultaneously make sure that agility work and sprint work adjusts to their bodies new configuration.

For athletes trying to gain mass at the appropriate time, there is often the misconception that simply lifting heavier weights will increase mass. Lifting heavy weights with low repetitions will not maximize size gains, although it can and will lead to mass gains. Canadian researchers showed in a study published in the Journal of Physiology, that leg extensions performed slowly, so as to maximize time under tension, produced "greater increases in rates of muscle protein synthesis than the same movement performed rapidly[85]."

In a bodybuilding workout, the trainer works to break down the muscles and to break down the muscles is to adhere to a principle called "time under tension." Time under tension is the amount of time the body is working under stress due to exercise. Doing push-ups for 10 seconds means my time under tension is 10 seconds, 20 seconds of squats is 20 seconds of time under tension, etc. Bodybuilding or time under tension workouts do not need to be very long, and I don't recommend using them for extended periods of time. During these workouts the muscles are taxed, broken down, and the lactic acid build-up is significant. They require significant rest post workout and proper protein intake. If an athlete uses bodybuilding workouts too often, he'll burn out, break down more muscle than he'll build up, see very little in terms of muscle mass gains, and likely get injured.

I recommend utilizing a variety of body building workouts as a change up in a workout training program for no longer than two weeks. For instance, I usually start off any body building sequence with the 10-20-10-20 workout. I start with this workout because a lot of athletes who come to me looking for weight gain have been doing one weight training program for an extended period of time. They haven't introduced much variety, if any at all into their workouts. This 10-20 (the short-hand term) workout helps confuse the muscles and forces the athletes to train differently. The workout is:

Pull-ups 10 reps
Push-ups 20 reps
Body Pulls 10 reps
Dips on Bench 20 reps
Drop 1 rep and repeat until reaching zero reps on pull-ups and body pulls
OR until every exercise hits zero.

How can a calisthenics workout, with no added weight for resistance, help build mass? The 10-20 workout helps most athletes because it shocks their muscles, confuses them, and breaks them down. Most athletes never do calisthenics workouts (not as flashy as weight training and definitely tougher). Athletes will do plenty of bicep curls and seated row exercises, but will neglect calisthenics.

What is unfortunate about the majority of training methods used today is they are not holistic. They treat the human body like it can be broken up into different parts and trained separately, yet expect the whole thing to operate synergistically. Does that make any sense? No.

Many athletes have problems with the 10-20-10-20 workout. They might be able to lift a lot on a lat pull down or seated row exercises (one works the lat muscles while the other works the rhomboids or upper back muscles) but when executing a pull-up, the core is important in stabilizing you're the body. Many athletes doing this workout have trouble keeping their body from swinging while doing pull-ups. That's less an arm strength issue and more of a stabilizer/core issue. This shows the training very quickly that while the athlete may be strong, he or she lacks functional holistic strength. This workout often creates soreness in the core the next day because the pull-ups and push-ups require core activation to be done properly. I recommend calisthenics workouts to younger pre-puberty athletes as a safer alternative to weight lifting.

Bodybuilding with weights should be done under careful supervision. Lactic acid build-up will occur, and athletes have a tendency to use incorrect form to complete repetitions and sets. Body building workouts utilize a couple specific repetition schemes and rest/work ratios. To build mass, generally use repetitions for each given exercise of at least eight repetitions. However, this depends on how much rest is allotted between sets. The goal is to maximize time under tension, which requires a balance between increasing the amount of time and tension an athlete can handle. As weight increases, the amount of repetitions an athlete can do decreases. As repetitions increase (assuming weight is constant), the amount of rest required also increases. The point at which the highest number of repetitions, least amount of rest, and highest amount of weight intersect is the point of highest time under tension.

An example of a bodybuilding set will increase back muscle mass is below:

> Bent Over Rows 12 reps
> Lat Pull Downs 12 reps
> Seated Rows 12reps
> Body Pulls of 12reps
> Rest and Repeat 3x

Start out with fewer repetitions, if needed. Or, drop the repetitions down to eight or five and allot less rest or no rest at all. Again, the point behind the workout is to increase muscle mass gains. Two smaller bodybuilding set examples are below:

> Bicep Curls 5 reps each arm
> Two Armed Dumbbell Hammer Curls 10 reps
> Wrist Curls 40 reps
> Repeat 3x

> Or the Triceps

> Tricep Push-Downs 10 reps
> Tricep Angled Push-Downs 15 reps
> Dips on Bench 20 reps
> Repeat 3x

Athletes can perform one exercise at a time in a way that helps tear down the muscles and promotes mass gains. For example, athletes can use resistance bands. When doing the bench press the resistance bands will increase resistance throughout the lift. Athletes can also do pulse repetitions whereby they only perform the first three to six inches of a given exercise movement. On the bench press this means bringing the dumbbells from their starting point at the chest and up about three to six inches and then back down. This requires the athlete to stabilize the weight and control it better. Furthermore, it keeps the athlete in time under tension and helps promote muscle breakdown. This is one of the best ways to gain weight, if the athlete meets the proper criteria: 1) physically mature, and 2) has regularly lifted weights and understands the lifts. The greatest danger when training for muscle mass is an athlete is not physically mature, hasn't spent much time lifting and doesn't understand proper lifting techniques.

Weight Training to Build Strength & Explosiveness

Hockey athletes should not singularly focus on gaining mass. Instead, they should utilize weight training to build a foundation of strength, explosiveness, and power. When training for strength, generally begin at eight repetitions or fewer (even as low as one repetition). Training for explosiveness requires an athlete push at 100 percent of his or her physical potential for each repetition. I recommend not exerting above five repetitions. If the weight is sufficiently high, five repetitions of explosive work will tax an athlete. Going higher requires using much less weight or a reduction in the force an athlete can apply to the weight.

How does building strength and explosiveness in the weight room relate to hockey? A hockey player obviously needs strength to improve and excel in the sport. Strong legs will keep players from getting knocked off the puck. It's difficult to win battles in the corner with weak lower body strength. Explosiveness is even more important than strength, I believe. The ability to quickly and powerfully check another player and then gain possession of the puck is a good skill to possess. It is one that requires not only pure strength, but also power and explosiveness. Explosiveness is also essential to hockey because the game is so often a battle of short sprints. The ability to go from zero to a hundred is essential. Yet, I still find the gains from weight training to be limited. All exercises in the weight room are contained in what Jack Blatherwick describes as a "barrel." An athlete stays relatively stationary – inside a barrel – when executing the bench press, squat, hang clean, or snatch. There is movement and benefits to those exercises, but the athlete's torso stays in a barrel throughout all the movements.

When training for strength and explosiveness, there are some key exercises I believe relate well to hockey. The most important among them is the squat. Vertical jump height is highly correlated with on-ice skating speed and off-ice sprint speed. The higher and more explosive an athlete jumps, the more likely the athlete will be faster, too. Imagine the first half of a squat jump – the player gets into the squat position and explodes upward. Without weight, a hockey player contends with his own mass and gravity. A clean and explosive squat is similar to the first half of the squat jump, but it adds additional resistance to the movement.

Often with hockey athletes I will have them squat with heavy weight three to five times in an explosive manner. They will slowly control the weight of their bodies down to the "pocket position." This occurs when the athlete squats to just below a 90 degree angle that forms between the thigh and shin. After hitting the pocket, the athlete explodes up to the starting position, careful not to come up on the toes. After performing these repetitions with heavy weight, athletes can "unload" and do three additional jumps. The idea is to trick your muscles and have them get used to a higher weight before bringing the weight back to normal so that it feels easier than before. This is similar to an athlete that skates with a weight vest and then takes it off to work on sprint training.

Another important exercise for hockey players is the one legged squat or lunge squat. An athlete puts weight over the shoulders (preferably in the form of plyo-tubes) and squats on one leg while holding the other leg on top of a bench. The benefits of this are expanded; athletes who hold weight over their shoulders, balance on one leg, and squat to a 90 degree position will not be easy to knock off the puck. Other weight room exercises like the push press, hang cleans, and snatches are great for training explosiveness and strength. To provide some context, see explosiveness focused and strength focused sample workouts below:

SAMPLE SIMPLE STRENGTH WORKOUT

Squats 3 sets of 8 reps
w/Pull Ups 3 sets of 8 reps

Bench Press 3 sets of 8 reps
w/Hamstring curls 3 sets of 8 reps

Tricep Push Downs 3 sets of 8 reps
One-legged Leg Press 3 sets of 8 reps each leg
DB Incline Bench Press 3 sets of 8 reps
Lat Pull Downs 3 sets of 8 reps

SAMPLE EXPLOSIVENESS FOCUSED WORKOUT

Push-Press 3x of 5 reps
w/ Front Planks 3 sets of 1 minute

One-armed Snatch 3x of 5 reps each arm
w/ Leg Raises 3 sets of 25 reps

Explosive Thrusters 3x of 5 reps
Explosive Step Ups w/Weight 3x of 5reps
Kneeling Cleans 3x of 5 reps

The sample strength workout uses two major lifts (squats and bench press) and supersets them with lifts that work different muscle groups. After completing the two main lifts move to the secondary lifts (four in total). This is a simple, straightforward workout template.

    The explosiveness focused sample workout has a total of five explosive exercises. For clarification, thrusters are where an athlete has dumbbells rested at shoulder length. The athlete squats slowly, explodes into the standing position, and simultaneously presses the dumbbells toward the ceiling. Kneeling cleans are where an athlete literally cleans the bar from a kneeling position to a standing one. A very difficult exercise! For each exercise above, the key is to train explosiveness at 100%. It is imperative to have a professional trainer assist athletes in a workout like this. Among many other reasons is the fact that the athlete needs someone to monitor his or her ability to employ force at 100%. A good trainer can see when an athlete is no longer able to exert at 100% of his or her potential and will change focus of the workout or stop it altogether.

The benefits from this type of strength and explosiveness training are good, but hockey specific plyometrics, that are explained later, are far more relatable to the game. Strength training has other benefits for hockey players. Building muscle strength in the weight room, if done properly, can help an athlete build a well-rounded and physically tuned body. Weak muscle groups can be trained to be stronger and more equivalent to surrounding muscle groups so as to help prevent injury. For instance, a lot of hockey players suffer from shoulder separations and shoulder impingements. Shoulder impingement happens when the shoulder rotates forward and inward, causing pain in the shoulder joint. This occurs often with hockey players because back training isn't done properly. Training the chest provides more visible "results" for coaches at the expense or neglect of the rhomboids and lat muscles. The back muscles surrounding the scapula help in maintaining a proper posture. The seated row exercise, for instance, works to help pull the shoulder muscles back and strengthens the rhomboid muscles that connect the scapula with the vertebrae of the spinal column.

    Strength and explosiveness training in the weight room are beneficial to hockey athletes. They provide a solid foundation for athletic movements and help prevent injury by strengthening important muscle groups. Most weight training, however, compartmentalizes the different muscles groups. Athleticism is the synergy of muscular strength across the entire body so while strength and explosiveness training is important for hockey, its utility must be put in perspective.

The Need to Think Outside the Box

Innovation in any field requires an open mind and willingness to question, be critical, and analyze even the most commonly held assumptions. It requires a philosophy that is grounded in an "outside-the-box" mentality. Remember the cheerleading team where we designed a training program tailored to the sport instead of using a training ideology? We utilized an "outside-the-box" approach to come up with a completely tailored training program. For too long, athletic trainers have espoused the same training philosophies instead of continually examining and re-examining training methods for a given sport. As I've already mentioned, I believe there is an overemphasis on weight training and complacent acceptance among the athletic training community on its effectiveness in training athleticism.

Football is probably the team sport where weight training is the most effective in promoting on field success. Every year the NFL holds a combine where it puts players through a variety of different tests and drills. These help scouts evaluate the up and coming stars of the NFL. It seems reasonable to assume those who perform the best in the combines also will perform very well in the NFL. Yet, that's not the case. We know combines are poor predictors of future success for NFL players. An article in the *Wall Street Journal* notes:

> *"According to a recent study by economists at the University of Louisville, there's no 'consistent statistical relationship' between the results of players at the Combine and subsequent NFL performance*[86]*."*

The Harvard Sports Analysis blog conducted statistical analysis on combine measurements and specific positions to determine what, if anything, can predict future success. They used a metric, Career Approximate Value (CAV), to attempt to find correlations between combine results and on-field success. Even with the extensive analysis they performed, they concluded the "models are still very weak" and "at best explain 21% of the variance in production at a given position (for defensive positions)[87]." Their analysis for offensive positions produced some significant results, but again, the models didn't account for much of the variance in future performance. For example, height and shuttle speed were significant when correlated with quarterback performance, but they only explained "5% of the variance in quarterback performance[88]."

The fundamental problem with the indicators from combines is they do not test athleticism. The bench press, squat, shuttle run, and vertical jump all test elements of athleticism, but do not simulate the full spectrum of qualities an athlete needs to be considered athletic. Height and shuttle speed are important for a quarterback to be successful, but effectiveness at that position seems to be the combination of so many other factors. What about poise and restraint? Those attributes are parts of a complex algorithm that makes up an athlete and are especially important at the quarterback position.

Athleticism is the ability to synchronize speed, endurance, quickness, explosiveness, strength, coordination, and power in an intelligent manner that allows an athlete to overcome diverse and unpredictable situations with multiple solutions. In other words, athleticism is *complex*. Athleticism is not simply being able to do a set of skills under a finite amount of situations. True athleticism is adaptable to different situations. It is imaginative and creative, not repetitive and monotonous. The combine looks to compartmentalize athleticism and test each attribute by itself – speed, quickness, agility, strength, etc. Some of the tests for individual attributes, like the bench press for strength, may not be accurate approximations of strength. Functional strength in hockey, for example, requires the synergy between the upper body, core, and legs. An athlete with a disproportionally weak core may be able to do a lot on the bench press, but how well will he or she be able to check an opponent or receive a hit?

To be fair, athleticism requires motor skills that are specific to a given sport. Elite basketball players will have shot thousands of baskets in their driveways growing up. This is necessary to build single dimension skill sets. But the game – whether it is basketball or hockey or football – requires athleticism, not just the execution of a skill under confined parameters. Blatherwick wrote an article describing how having hockey skills is not sufficient to be a great hockey player. He writes, "Hockey is a game of quick decisions, many of them spontaneous and creative. We cannot possibly anticipate every decision and tell players in advance what to do in every situation[89]." That is why it's easy to measure tests for bench pressing or speed skating, but these tests do not accurately portray the ability of the player. Perhaps someday, with advanced technologies, there will be tests that are variable enough to provide coaches and scouts with more accurate information.

Training for Speed, Quickness, and Agility

Speed, quickness, and agility are the key athletic attributes that make a great hockey player. Strength and endurance can be improved into adulthood whereas athleticism gains become much harder to realize. Also, strength is a poor substitute for speed. At the elite levels, all skaters are fast. It's a pre-requisite to playing the game. Strength can vary far more than speed. As I said earlier, if an athlete is quick and has speed, a scout will see potential. If a hockey player is big, strong, and slow, a scout will see a lost opportunity.

Before detailing the ways an athlete can build speed, quickness, and agility. I'll define each term. Speed is how fast someone can skate. Quickness is how fast top speed is reached. There are some skaters who are fast, but not quick, and, similarly, some skaters who are quick, but not fast. Generally, in a relative sense taller hockey players with long legs are fast, but not as quick and shorter players are quick, but not as fast. Differentiating between speed and quickness is especially important when training different body types. A quick forward that is great in the corners, but always seems to be behind on the back check needs to work on speed, not quickness. Agility is the ability to combine quickness with changes in direction and speed (deceleration and acceleration) at any given time. Agility is as much about the ability to start, as it is to stop.

The importance of speed, quickness, and agility cannot be underestimated in hockey. Yet, this is not the focus of many strength training programs in high school. Training to skate explosively is mentally difficult. When training for speed and quickness there is one very important principle: *in order to become faster, an athlete must sprint at 100 percent*. To sprint or perform agility drills at 100 percent, athletes need rest.

The results of the Wingate Anaerobic Test show how to train at 100 percent and also the need for rest to maximize training gains. The Wingate Anaerobic Test is conducted on a stationary resistance bike where power output is recorded. A study published in the "Journal of Strength and Conditioning Research" showed that Max Power Output values "are reached within five to six seconds of the start of the test and are sustained for no longer than 3 to 4 seconds[90]." This study conducted a 10-second Wingate Test and a 30-second Wingate Test. In the first case, the subjects reached maximal power output, but in the latter test they didn't. Top-notch athletes couldn't hold 100 percent for more than a few seconds and they could only achieve maximum speed during the 10-second set. In the 30-second test, these athletes never reached their top velocity because they, likely subconsciously, knew they had to conserve some energy in order to finish the 30 seconds at a high speed. Young hockey players are most likely unable to train at 100 percent when drills last for more than 10-seconds too. Mental toughness training through difficult endurance tasks can be valuable. However, if done during skating, this training can result in bad form and a negative impact on skating dynamics.

In order to recover quickly from fast sprints and to actually sprint 100 percent, it is important to keep sprints under 15 seconds and preferably under 10 seconds. On the right is a graph that I've taken from Jack Blatherwick's book *Overspeed Skills Training for Hockey* that demonstrates the amount of lactate buildup and glycogen depletion that occurs during different work to rest intervals[91]. The ratio is consistent at one second of work to two seconds of rest. This research shows the longer the work, the greater the lactic acid build-up, even though the rest to work ratios stays the same.

Intermittent work at 400 watts
Muscle metabolites vs. Time

Lactate Buildup / Glycogen Depletion

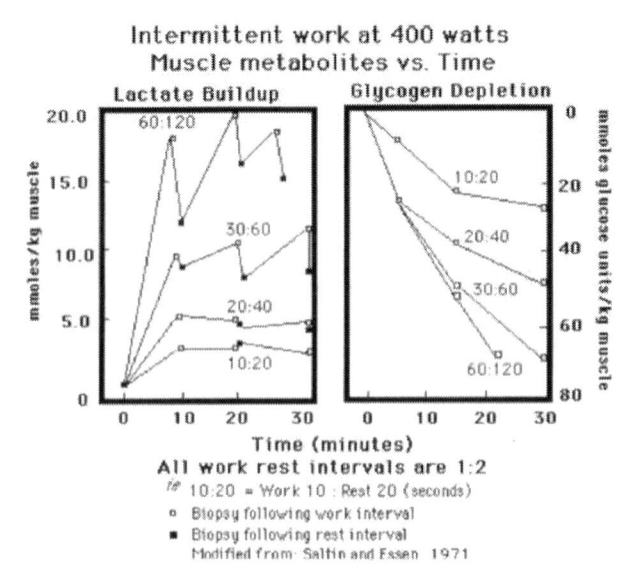

Time (minutes)
All work rest intervals are 1:2
10:20 = Work 10 : Rest 20 (seconds)
○ Biopsy following work interval
■ Biopsy following rest interval
Modified from: Saltin and Essen 1971

Source Blatherwick, Jack. OVERSPEED: Skill Training for Hockey
<http://burnsvillehockey.com/DevOverspeed.html>.

In the beginning of a training program for speed, it is important to use short sprints and long recovery times. This will help keep down the amount of lactic acid buildup and will not deplete glycogen stores too quickly. After athletes get into shape, the sprint length can increase and rest ratios can decrease. What will occur as athletes get into better shape is they'll deal with the lactic acid buildup from sprinting better and their heart rate will recover faster from the sprint. As we progress in a program designed to increase speed it is simultaneously working on endurance! More importantly, there is hockey specific endurance. Hockey is a game of short sprints and longer rest intervals. At the youth ranks, if there are three lines the rest to work ratio is at least 1:3 (remember, with whistles, time outs, etc. the ratio is far greater). In college the ratio can widen as most schools play four lines. When training to sprint and recover, the actions are emulating more closely how hockey is played.

If training for speed is sprinting as fast as possible, how does one train for quickness? In the Wingate Test, it took the subjects about five to six seconds to reach their maximum power output or maximum speed. When training for quickness, the primary concern is how quickly an athlete can reach top speed. Athletes tested in this study were world class athletes and so less trained athletes may take longer to reach full speed. The goal of quickness training is to get an athlete to be extremely explosive in the first few steps of sprinting or skating stride and to reach full speed quickly thereafter. The goal of speed training is to reach top speed, hold it for as long as possible, and stop.

Applying this principle to agility training is important, too. It's too easy to run agility drill after agility drill with little rest until everyone in the workout is exhausted. The coach or trainer does little and it looks like a great workout since everyone is huffing and puffing. The problem is the athletes aren't becoming more agile. They are simply getting a cardio workout. They might as well be sent on a jog. Agility training should have sufficient rest to work ratios so athletes can exert at 100 percent every single time. Beyond that, all agility training only requires a little creativity. See Chapter 5 for examples of agility drills.

Core Training: The Missing Link

Core training is extremely important for hockey players. I think it is in some aspects more important than upper body strength. Everything starts with the legs, but to maximize leg strength and upper body strength, core training is essential. At the same time, hockey players who do core training often go through core circuits, and a variety of core exercises for a specified period of time, until they've taxed the core muscles. This isn't bad; I put core training like this into many of my athlete's programs. What I think is missed, however, is the synergistic role the core plays. Imagine a hockey player skating down the ice. He is about to get hit, so he moves to the side and becomes slightly off balance. The opposing player hits him clean at the shoulder. The hit isn't direct, but it is pretty hard. If the athlete has a strong core that can hold the upper body and leg strength in unison, then he'll continue to stand up. However, if the core is very weak, he'll fall. Also, imagine the activation of the core simply when doing agile movements. It helps stabilize the torso and keeps advanced movements controlled.

It is important to note that core training isn't just the abdominal muscles. Many athletes tend to think of the core very narrowly. For hockey players especially, training the lower back through back extensions, proper squats, supermans, and other exercises helps not only prevent injury, but also keep the body stable.

I separate core training workouts into three types: endurance, stability, and strength. Endurance core training can best be understood as a traditional core circuit. An example is an athlete working six minutes on sit-ups, crunches, leg raises, etc. For hockey players, endurance core training also can work the very important hip flexors. Exercises that require athletes to lift their legs and activate the core (like leg raises, butterfly kicks, etc.) activate the hip flexor muscles. Endurance training is important so an athlete's core can maintain strength throughout a game. A weak core increases the risk of injury.

Stability training requires the athlete to maintain posture by using the abdominal muscles. One of the simplest stability exercises is the front or side plank. From my experience with high school athletes, many of them do not have strong stabilizer muscles. When I started training football players, I incorporated a front plank into every warm up. Over the course of the summer the front plank would get longer and longer. At the start, it was amazing how difficult a simple, 30-second front plank was for the players. The big lineman had the toughest time. They were so top and bottom heavy that their cores sank to the floor. Having weak stabilizer muscles increases the likelihood they will get injured, and reduces a player's *functional strength*. Think again about the scenario with the hockey player skating down the ice, weaving through traffic, etc. Without strong core stabilizer muscles it is hard to stay balanced and utilize upper and lower body strength.

Strength training for the core is usually done with weights and includes exercises like cable twists (also good for stability), woodchoppers, and weighted crunches. Core strength training is probably more neglected than stability training. However, it is an important part of training the core. Many core strength exercises like cable twists help replicate motions used in hockey. Cable twists or oblique twists help strengthen muscles used when shooting the puck. These exercises require the use of core stabilizers, too.

Plyometric and Skating Form Training

Two primary types of hockey specific training are plyometrics and skating form training. Plyometrics are explosive jumping exercises that can be defined into two separate categories. Quick feet plyometrics emphasize the need for athletes to move their feet off the ground as fast as possible. These plyometrics generally start from a non-hockey position. Ankle bouncers, for example, are where an athlete stands up with the knee slightly bent and explodes upward using the calf muscles. The object is to hit the ground and explode up as fast as possible. Line drills are another example. An athlete quickly moves his or her feet from left to right, forward to back, on one leg or two, over an imaginary or drawn line on the ground. Again, the goal isn't to jump high, but to move the feet as quickly as possible. This type of plyometric training is important and it helps develop quick feet skills. However, a greater emphasis should be placed on developing explosiveness.

In hockey, players use their thighs and gluts to explode and skate. Plyometrics that are hockey specific work on building leg strength from a hockey position (90-degree angled squat). One example of a beneficial exercise to hockey players is the vertical jump. The player starts in a squat and explodes from that position to get as high in the air as possible. Another exercise is the broad jump where the athlete jumps and extends far forward. The similarities of leaning forward, jumping and a quick start on the ice are remarkable.

The other form of hockey specific training is known as skating form training. This type of training helps an athlete get into the proper hockey skating position and replicate skating movements. One of my favorite training exercises in this category is called skating lunges. In this exercise athletes move as if they are skating on ice. It's that simple. They get into a skating position and make strides like they are skating. If the exercise is done on a slippery surface it makes it even easier. What I've noticed is the way athletes perform skating lunges off the ice is quite similar to how they skate on it. The best skaters are the best at skating lunges. Those that do not extend fully, tend to also shorten their skating lunge prematurely.

How to Warm-Up Properly

Youth athletes tend to be very ignorant of the risks associated with athletic training. As a result, they generally do not warm-up properly, if at all. Most athletes think a warm-up is a jog around the track or a few minutes on the stationary bike. As long as they start sweating a little or get their heart rate up, they think they're ready to train/practice. A proper warm-up not only gets the heart rate up and the body warm, but it also increases the athlete's flexibility. The best way to warm-up is to do a dynamic warm-up where stretching takes place through active motion. Below is a sample warm-up:

1. Jog ¼ mile
2. Perform these exercises for 20 meters
   - High Knees
   - Butt Kicks
   - High Skips
   - Long Skips
   - Walking Lunges
   - Side Lunges

- Cherry Pickers
- Frankenstein Kicks
- Knee pulls
- IT Band Pulls
- Accelerator Sprints

3. Front Plank for 60 seconds
4. 10 push-ups
5. 10 deep squats with a wide stance
6. 30 seconds of arm circles

There are a lot of exercises in this warm-up. It takes about 15 minutes to complete, and for the out-of-shape athlete can be a workout in itself. The exercises performed over 20 meters help increase flexibility and range of motion. Front planks are great because they warm up the core's stabilizer muscles. It is important to warm up these muscles as they can pull or strain if not properly ready for heavy weight.

Leadership, Character, and Team Training in Hockey

Chapter 3

Introduction

In the beginning of the 20th century, sports were considered a substitute for war. The purpose was to replace the values war had taught young men with something more humane. Dr. Walter B. Canon was quoted in the *New York Times* in 1915 saying sports were a way to "satisfy the demand of strong men for the clash of strength against strength in opposition[92]." Instead of taking up arms against one another in combat, societies could release these war-like emotions on the sports field. Society would presumably benefit because sports help "produce valor, fortitude, self-control, [and] obedience to command –the virtues which are lauded by the militarists as the virtues bred by war[93]." Although sports haven't become a substitute for war, their stated purpose – to instill societal values – continues to this day.

Most people don't see sports as outlets for warlike aggression. Instead, sports are seen as beneficial in a multitude of ways: they help promote physical fitness in an increasingly overweight youth population, and they encourage teamwork, leadership, character, and life skills. Many athletes agree that sports help build character and develop positive values. Sports organizations often market themselves as activities for youth to develop life skills.

I believe there are many ways sports build character. Unfortunately, the emphasis on building character in sports seems to be weakening, especially in hockey. Everyone has heard the scandals concerning illegal drugs, cheating, fighting, and unsportsmanlike conduct in the professional ranks. These problems have manifested themselves at our colleges and high schools, too. As Tim Flannery, the associate director of the National Federation of State High School Associations in Indianapolis observed, "some of the problems we now have in high school sports mirror the problems they have at the professional and college level[94]." He went on to note that "we're all progressing down the same path...winning is becoming the most important thing[95]."

Learning to compete is one benefit hockey provides young athletes. That spirit and drive to compete, and to win, is what helps people become successful. The problem is when winning becomes something greater than maintaining a strong character, the entire definition of winning has changed. Winning is about defeating another opponent in a manner that is consistent with the spirit of competition.

The process of professionalization in sports at younger ages has degraded the value placed upon character and ethics. Sports have become more about making the best team than being the best teammate. Parents in the stands disparage young hockey players when they make a bad pass or skate too slow. Youth athletes will pick up on this and begin to think that they too can talk bad about their teammates. It is not too much of an exaggeration to say that the future of thousands of young athletes depends on us changing the culture that surrounds youth sports. To do that, we need to make a conscious effort to promote leadership, team, and character training into our hockey programs and community associations. Instead of the ice rink being a place where young athletes learn a "me-first" mentality, it should be one that adds to their development! The rink can and should be considered a classroom in which youth athletes develop physical, emotional, and academic skills. To make this a reality, the entitlement culture must stop.

The Entitlement Culture

The most pervasive and perhaps negative value our sports culture is teaching young athletes is entitlement. Often, when a player doesn't make a team, parents respond fairly angrily to the selection committee and program leaders. They almost always feel the process was "politicized" or unfair. Sometimes parents even move to different cities to get a fresh start.

Many angry parents think their son or daughter had been unfairly treated. Most of the time, they are wrong. Generally, in these cases a player was close to making the more advanced team and was one of the last few cut. In these circumstances, it is generally better for the player to play as one of the top few players on the B team as opposed to one of the worst on the A team. Especially in a team sport like hockey, playing at a lower level can be very advantageous for players because it can help them learn new skills, see the ice better, and slow the game down.

However, even if we assume a parent's complaint is legitimate (which they can be), the response should be to work hard and persevere. Unfair assessments at work, grading in college, and in other life circumstances happen all the time. It's important our youth understand that when life doesn't go their way, they must look for solutions instead of whining.

What is ironic about unethical behavior in sports is it has been fueled by a desire to win at all costs yet leads to more losses than anything else. Hockey is a game of synergy where the sum of the abilities of the players on the ice is greater than the whole, if they work together. This is lost when athletes think teams are designed to serve their "interests." Isn't a key requirement for success working with others? Some people make millions (some billions) because they are brilliant at leveraging the talents and strengths of others. Students need to learn these interpersonal skills and hockey provides coaches and parents a great opportunity to teach them.

When John Wooden described his success as a coach, he understood that had he not won so many games and national championships at UCLA, people would not have considered him successful. Coach Wooden did not see his success as the number of wins his teams achieved on the court, but rather the successes his players had after the game. He proudly remarked in a documentary about his life available that most of his players became extremely successful persons later in life[96]. It is these achievements Coach Wooden valued most and hoped his efforts helped produce.

No matter the athlete, someday everyone will lace up his or her skates. Teaching strong character, teamwork, and leadership skills are important for everyone. I think the following lessons are very applicable to the game of hockey and life in general. By no means is this an exhaustive list, but I hope it provides some insight into the benefits hockey can have for youth athletes.

Transactional and Transformative Leadership in Sports

There are two distinct categories of leadership in sports. The first type is known as transactional leadership. Transactional leadership is leading a group of people to accomplish a given task. The focus is on the task more than on the interaction between leader and teammates. This task might be leading the team through a structured warm up or insuring everyone watches a movie together as a team bonding event. Transactional leadership can start when athletes are very young. To an adult, tasks like leading a warm up may seem trivial, but they are important first steps for young athletes developing leadership abilities.

To successfully execute a simple task like running a warm up, the athlete must be assertive, take responsibility, and communicate commands effectively. Athletes need to be given the opportunity to perform leadership tasks like leading warm-up. Transactional leadership is the building block for more complicated forms of leadership and many of its aspects should be expected by all teammates. A player as young as 10 years old can lead a warm up or ensure the locker-room is clean after a game. Part of being a good teammate is the ability to take responsibility for the actions of the team.

Transformational leadership is completely different from transactional and is much harder to teach and to do. Transformational leadership requires a level of understanding most athletes don't quite acquire until they are in their teens. Although this doesn't mean it can't be taught, in an elementary form, with younger athletes. Transformational leadership seeks to solve a problem, and leverage a group's abilities so they resolve issues more effectively. This type of leadership takes a team and makes it cohesive, leverages strengths, and covers weaknesses. A transformational leader will reach out to a teammate who might be struggling and through his or her leadership *improves* the teammate's performance. This leadership requires the ability to see problems, and not simply execute tasks. It also requires the athlete to understand how to communicate with others effectively, to inspire teammates to work harder for a common goal, and to encourage the team when they're down.

Imagine a game where one of the defenseman on the team isn't doing very well. She makes a terrible pass to the center of the ice in the defensive zone that results in a goal and two shifts later uncharacteristically goes too far into the offensive zone, resulting in the opposing team scoring another goal. She's a good player, but right now she's obviously not playing very well.

Unfortunately, a typical reaction by teammates might be to ridicule or talk about their friend behind her back. If the team loses, parents and players might claim, "Janelle really lost the game for us today with her terrible defensive play." Or, "if only Janelle had showed up tonight, we'd have won the game!" Obviously, these reactions are the exact opposite of what a transformational leader will do. She might go up to Janelle after the second mistake (better yet, after the first one), and tell her: "Janelle, we need you out there. Keep your head up, forget the past, and re-focus. Don't worry about that last one, nothing you can do about it now. If we are going to have a chance of winning this game, we need you on board 100 percent." This can be the difference between a win or loss, and in the context of an entire season, the difference between winning a championship or just getting close. In fact, it is impossible for a team to achieve its full potential without transformational leadership.

Teaching transformational leadership is not easy and parents can start teaching transformational leadership by leading by example. One thing no athlete, coach or parent should do is trash talk fellow teammates. It is not right and it shouldn't be tolerated. Use the examples given above to exercise transformational leadership skills. Go through sport scenarios and talk through how to react to them with leaders. Knowing when to exercise leadership is tough; it takes practice. When I look back on the time I was a captain, I think of all the opportunities I had to lead, but simply didn't know fully what to do. In hindsight, I can think of ways I should have reacted to certain situations. If I had thought through some of these difficult situations, I would have been better prepared.

Consider these sports leadership scenarios:

> Scenario 1: Your team hasn't performed well lately. In fact, you've lost the last three games. No one has given up yet, but there is a pessimistic mood that permeates throughout the team. A couple teammates start to complain about the coaching, and a few others feel the couple players who aren't performing well enough are the reason for the losses. Players who aren't playing well seem to be losing confidence. The next game is in a few days. How would you react?
>
> Scenario 2: Your team is doing great. You've won your last five games and everyone is happy. However, practices aren't as intense as they were earlier in the season and you start to sense some players are being complacent. The next game is against a weak opponent and players are already making fun of the competition. What would you do in this situation?
>
> Scenario 3: Your team is close, except for one group. This group hangs out together and is rumored to drink. The season is going well, but you feel the team isn't a cohesive group. How could you pull everyone together?
>
> Scenario 4: A few players are drinking. One of them is a really great player and helps the team win. The other two don't get much playing time. The playoffs are in two weeks. What do you do?
>
> Scenario 5: Classmates and a few teammates are bullying one of the weaker players on your team at school. What should you do?

Sports aren't complicated. The same issues occur year after year at every level. Some teams get too confident and lose focus, and others become negative and spiral out of control. By going over sports scenarios like these, issues are rehearsed that almost certainly will come up during the season.

Today, great teaching is more accessible than at any other time in the history of humankind. The internet provides a platform for many educational resources to be made available to people for free. Utilize open source leadership training tools such as TED.com. For instance, Simon Sinek has a TED presentation titled "How great leaders inspire action." In this training, he describes a simple, but extremely powerful principle: The Why, How, What principle. This principle is important for transformational leaders. It states that people are motivated by why a leader or organization wants to accomplish a goal and not so much interested in how that goal will be accomplished or even what it is. This principle is irrelevant to a transactional leader running a warm up. But for a high school hockey captain trying to get his team to the state championship, this is an incredibly relevant principle. TED.com has many other good tools including Stanley McChrystal's "Listen, learn…then lead." John Wooden also gives a presentation on TED regarding true success.

The Power of Determined Optimism

    Tom Rath, author of *How Full is Your Bucket*, writes about the power of optimism and how it changes outcomes and results. To illustrate the importance of positivity and the destructiveness of negativity, he cites an interesting study conducted by Major (Dr.) William E. Mayer of POW Camps after the Korean War. The American soldiers at these POW camps were given food and shelter. There was very little physical abuse; "in fact fewer cases of physical abuse were reported in the North Korean POW camps than in prison camps from any other major military conflict throughout history[97]." At first glance, one might think that given these relatively kinder conditions that the survival rate from the POW camps would have been very high. However, the opposite occurred. The camps had the highest death rate in American military history, an astonishing 38%[98].

    How could this happen? The answer is profound: instead of physically abusing the inmates, the North Koreans employed a variety of psychological tortures. The Korean camp guards withheld all positive support, while inundating the soldiers with negative news. For example, "if a soldier received a supportive letter from home, the captors withheld it" whereas "all negative letters were delivered to soldiers immediately[99]." Prisoners were rewarded for breaking ranks with each other and snitching on their fellow soldiers. The guards would force every prisoner, in front of his comrades, to criticize himself. Ultimately, the camp guards looked to break down the loyalty the prisoners felt to each other, their leadership within the camp, and their country. This negative atmosphere was incredibly deadly as "half of [the] soldiers died simply because they had given up[100]."

The North Korean POW camps demonstrate that being positive and supporting teammates is absolutely crucial to team success. In a POW camp it is a matter of life and death. On a hockey team, it is the difference between winning a state championship and not making it past the first round of playoffs. I have often told this story to hockey players and teams. The reason: hockey has become so competitive that sometimes teammates and even coaches fight each other just as much as they fight the opponents. In fact, as a study by F. Clark Power demonstrates, one out of five coaches admits to contributing to a negative culture by teasing the less skilled players on their teams[101].

Coaches, parents, and players should understand that negativity toward teammates only produces a reduction in performance. At some point, those players who feel the negativity might lessen their performances and/or give up on the team altogether. The drive to win at all costs (even costs to our character and principles) ultimately destroys teams and hurts their chances of success.

Taking Criticism Well

One problem with the current sports culture is youth athletes aren't being taught how to take criticism well. This, in turn, will affect their future success in sports, in the classroom, and in the workforce. It is through criticism (instruction), that we improve and become better.

Criticism is not inherently negative or positive – regardless of the intent of the individual supplying it. It is a player's reaction to criticism that makes it either positive or negative. If a player does not receive adequate criticism, he or she will inevitably fall behind. For example, the best players at any given level have weaknesses that often are masked by their strengths. A young hockey player that is remarkably fast and quick will not have to worry about stick handling until other players can skate at similar speeds. He or she may not develop this skill properly without constructive criticism.

John Wooden, one of the greatest coaches of all time, taught his players: "a man may make mistakes, but he isn't a failure until he starts blaming someone else[102]." What is important is lessons are learned from mistakes. Learning to learn from mistakes is not easy. We naturally want to be right and when we aren't we tend to fight back. Hockey is such a great vehicle to help teach young boys and girls how to deal with failure and criticism. It's a shame that often players are shielded from harsh, but necessary truths that would ultimately benefit them.

Communication Principles for Leaders and Great Teammates

Dale Carnegie wrote a great book in the 1930s titled *How to Win Friends and Influence People*. In it, he provides nine principles for successful communication[103]. Understanding these principles is a big part of being a great leader. More specifically, these principles are the fundamentals for a transformational leader to understand. It is through effective communication with teammates and coaches that transformational leaders can often have the biggest impact. Although the principles Dale Carnegie conveyed were written for business professionals, they also apply to sports. Below are his nine principles:

Principle 1: Begin with praise and honest appreciation
Principle 2: Call attention to people's mistakes indirectly
Principle 3: Talk about your own mistakes before criticizing the other person
Principle 4: Ask questions instead of giving direct orders
Principle 5: Let the other person save face
Principle 6: Praise the slightest improvement and praise every improvement. Be "hearty in your approbation and lavish in your praise."
Principle 7: Give the other person a fine reputation to live up to
Principle 8: Use encouragement. Make the fault seem easy to correct.

Principle 9: Make the other person happy about doing the thing you suggest

Carnegie's approach can be summed up nicely: approach others with respect, praise them genuinely, and guide others with dignity instead of shame. This approach doesn't come naturally, but the game of hockey provides a great learning ground for young leaders to test their skills.

The Value of Hard Work

Hard work sounds simple, right? It is obviously important and necessary for success. Yet, teaching hard work is not easy. It is one of the hardest values to teach youth athletes. A 10-year old youth hockey player has a definition of hard work that is different from that of a high school hockey player; and similarly, a college player's definition of hard work is different than that of most high school players. As players age they learn "new" definitions of hard work. They realize they can push themselves farther and as they do they gradually expand their understanding of what it means to truly work hard.

Hard work is something all coaches want to instill in their athletes. With it, their athletes can achieve success in a variety of different domains – from hockey to school to work. Despite the importance of hard work, teaching it is something we as coaches probably haven't put enough thought to. To start, what is the definition of hard work? And second, how do we teach it?

I define hard work during training, because it is easier to identify through experience than words. For instance, after most, if not all, of the athletes hit the point where they are thinking, "it would be nice for this to be over now," I let them know the hard work has now started. Hard work in hockey begins when the majority of skaters start thinking about quitting. Before this point their efforts are simply average.

At any age group, the majority of athletes will place a limit on their potential. Generally, the younger the age, the greater the limit the athlete will place on himself or herself. When I coached girls' basketball, I told my players one day that I thought they were probably using less than 30 percent of their physical potential. They looked shocked because they thought they'd been working hard. They were working hard according to the definition they had defined for themselves, but not the one they were capable of.

Teaching hard work is a continuous process; it takes place over years, not months. Hard work can't be forced on students at ages where they are not ready to understand it. An eight year old hears hard work and has very little grasp of the concept. All the yelling and screaming in the world will only do harm. In hockey practices, coaches should point out when players have pushed outside their comfort zones or are moving their feet faster than they have ever before. By doing this, coaches highlight the new definition of hard work. They provide a tangible example the players can remember and refer to later on. Over time and with great patience, coaches will see tremendous gains in their player's abilities to work hard.

Humility and Loyalty

It's important to teach athletes humility. Instead of hockey players boasting about the teams they make or bragging about how many points they scored in the last game, they should be taught to accept success with a humble attitude. If a hockey player boasts about his or her play, it often means he or she is lacking in self-esteem. Great players don't need to boast about themselves, others will be more than happy to do so for them.

Humility is an incredibly important attribute, one often overlooked in our personality obsessed hockey culture. A team can accomplish amazing things when everyone is willing to do their part, regardless of the praise or recognition they are given. During my sophomore year of high school, the varsity team made it to the state quarterfinal game. The reason we made it to the tournament wasn't because of our superstars, it was primarily because we had players who, although they did not receive the glory or credit for our wins from the statisticians, were just as necessary and sometimes more so than our top scorers.

When a team is a true team it is full of humble individuals who are loyal to the team's success before any other consideration. What is ironic is the selfish and individualistic approach to sports – the "me-first" mentality – hurts the development of the player and the success of the team. I like to teach my players: $1 + 1 = 3$. If players don't work as a team, mathematically they can only equal, at best, two. However, if everyone plays together, leverages strengths and covers weaknesses, all become greater than the sum of the parts. The only way to achieve this synergy is if players are humble and loyal.

Leadership, character, and team training are important and essential aspects to hockey training. Hockey can be a vehicle through which young boys and girls learn hard work, perseverance, determination, humility, integrity, and teamwork. However, for this to be the case, the culture surrounding youth hockey must change. It is not only harming young hockey player's futures outside of the game, but is also in many cases reducing their likelihood of making it to the game's elite ranks. It's time to reclaim our game and change it for the better.

On-Ice Training: Sample Drills

Chapter 4

Introduction

The following sections cover on-ice training techniques and methods. This isn't a practice plan or an exact guide to running a practice for any team at any level. The complexities of different ages, levels of players, and idiosyncrasies of groups mean it is *impossible* to create a manual repeatable in its entirety. The intent of this chapter is to provide a framework to follow: 1) as a parent to obtain a better understanding of proper training techniques for hockey and, thus, be a more intelligent consumer 2) as a coach to use this information to improve practices and the skill development of players and 3) as a player to understand what skills and drills to practice to become a better hockey player.

When it comes to on-ice training it cannot be emphasized enough, especially to parents, that on-ice training should stress fundamentals and skill development. In the off-season a lot of great programs work on skating dynamics and specific skills like stick handling, shooting, and passing. During the regular season, a lot of teams decide they need to work on systems, power plays, breakouts, etc. What is so frustrating about this is sometimes parents talk about the game in "system oriented language." They might say, if only Coach would change up the power play, or if only he'd teach them how to do a break out properly. When teams are struggling, the issue is generally not systems. It's the skill level of the players. Even a good team shouldn't work a lot on systems. Is it better to have a faster and more skilled team by the end of the year, or one that has memorized a book of systems? I believe the former is better than the latter. The regular season should be a time for athletes to improve in practice and experiment in games. Too often, parents don't realize this. Especially on losing teams, they pressure the coach to win and most coaches take pressure to mean that they have do more – more systems work.

There are two different types of training that will be discussed in this chapter: Overspeed Training (with and without pucks) and Underspeed Training. When running developmental practices, keep the drills easy to understand and the focus on quality repetitions. There are no systems drills and very little "chalk talk." The focus is always on development; to maximize development the coach should detail the drills *prior* to practice, even for squirts. Although it should be noted that Overspeed and Underspeed training is primarily intended for use with older players. Younger players can be given a few drills to understand, and the older players should be expected to memorize a greater percentage of practice.

Overspeed Training

What is Overspeed Training? Overspeed implies a skater is moving so fast that he or she is outside his or her comfort level. It requires intense focus and concentration and is very hard to do. Overspeed Training helps an athlete become faster by pushing past perceived limits. For example, a lot of Overspeed drills utilize cross overs and changes of direction. To be successful in hockey, a player needs to be able to move fast north to south, but also east to west. This requires an ability to move down the rink and very quickly turn around without losing speed. Imagine a skater going down the right side of the rink as fast as possible and turning toward the middle of the rink, the turn radius will be pretty wide. The reason a skater can't stay at full speed while turning is because the force placed upon the legs (specifically the inner one) is too great to handle. Some athletes will stand up a bit to release the pressure off the legs and in so doing they increase the width of the turn radius. For an athlete this can actually feel faster than turning on a dime. The reason is when an athlete turns very quickly, no matter how good, he or she will lose some speed. However, by widening the turn radius it is possible to maintain close to top speed. Overspeed Training challenges an athlete to make turns quicker, faster, and with a lower center of gravity.

In many ways, the effectiveness of Overspeed Training rests in the hands of the coach. If executed improperly, Overspeed drills can harm the skating dynamics of an athlete and actually make the player a worse skater. How so, you might ask? When a skater goes 100 percent there is a buildup of lactic acid in the legs that occurs very quickly. In fact, lactic acid build-up can cause an athlete to slow down after only 10 seconds (as demonstrated by the Wingate Bicycle Tests). The reason this is so important to understand is because when the intent is to train for speed, it is essential to go as fast as physically possible. Remember, the intent is to push beyond the comfort zone. Doing this requires following two basic principles: First, sprints must be short. For most athletes that is less than 10 seconds. Second, recovery times need to be sufficient so the athlete can skate at 100 percent again. Too often coaches (especially in football) think a hard workout is one where athletes "sprint" at 80 percent or less for 20 minutes until they throw up. These workouts serve no other purpose than helping build mental toughness and perhaps some tolerance to lactic acid build-up. Difficult workouts that build-up significant lactic acid can help to increase mental toughness and build team unity, but do not help players develop speed or quickness. Sprint workouts that do incorporate sufficient rest can also be mentally challenging, albeit in a different manner. These sprint with rest workouts require the athlete to go 100 percent. There is no excuse for anything less.

    The coach's responsibility is to make sure that athletes are training at 100% but also to read and react to his or her players. Are they showing signs of physical exhaustion and we therefore need to increase our rest to work ratios? Do they seem unmotivated so we need to take a break or provide purpose to the drills? Perhaps the players are in better shape now, recovering quicker, and rest to work ratios need to decrease.

    Below are Overspeed drills. Parents, coaches, and hockey players will benefit from understanding the basic principles outlined above as well as the more detailed suggestions provided below. When I met with Coach Tom Saterdalen, the legendary Jefferson Jaguar Varsity hockey coach in Bloomington, MN, and asked him for advice on running a summer hockey camp, he told me it wasn't so important what drills I used, but rather how I executed them. Make sure a "failure is okay" environment where falling down while going 100 percent is acceptable, he said. Correct a young hockey player who does the drill wrong and make sure that enough coaches watch each drill to ensure quality. If the player doesn't have the fundamentals right, the drill isn't worthwhile.

The S Sprint Drill

Most of the drills described here aren't complicated to run and can be easily explained. Executing these drills properly is the difficult part. Coaches should stand below the top of the first circle and just above the bottom of the second circle. These are two areas of the drill where athletes are most likely to use improper form and often need a coach to help recognize mistakes. When going around the first circle, athletes need to stay low so they fully extend their blade on the crossover and keep the entire blade on the ice. A lot of younger athletes when doing crossovers will use the front half or less of their blade. They don't fully extend and since the front half the blade tends to dig into the ice, they create unnecessary friction (which in turn, slows them down). Another point to consider with crossovers is that they should be rhythmic. Many players will do a few choppy crossovers, stop, glide, and resume. Instead, they should focus on crossing over the entire time and doing so rhythmically. Skaters must remember to stay low, use the full blade, and fully extend every stride.

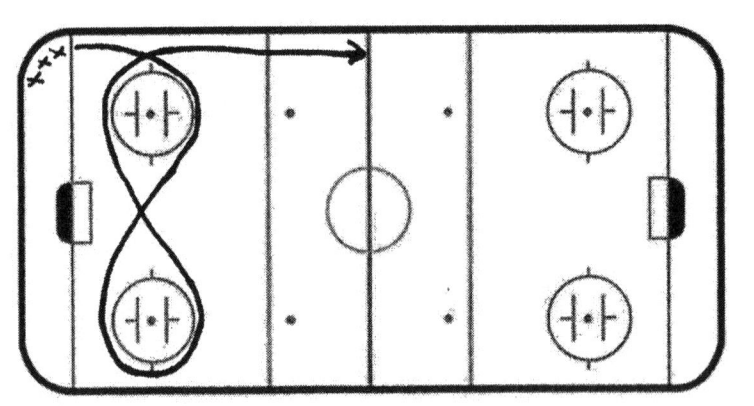

On the second circle the most important part of the drill occurs. The athletes have picked up speed and are moving very fast. The turn is pretty sharp and so the tendency is to slow down, stand up slightly, and shorten strides. Some athletes simply glide around the circle. Again, the athletes should push outside of their comfort zone, stay low, fully extend the blade, and keep their feet moving.

The Figure 8 Drill (short version)

This drill works on crossovers and the ability to keep athletes feet moving. Like the previous drill, place coaches inside the circles and instruct them to constantly provide feedback to the skaters as they go through the drill. Skating out of the last turn is the hardest part of the drill. It is essential athletes not stop moving their feet. The end of the drill is at mid ice. It is also beneficial if a coach is placed on the red line (mid ice) to watch the players as they skate by. The tendency for players is to stop striding and slow down by a fraction of a second just before the finish line. This is not acceptable because it means at best the player is skating at 99 percent. The last few strides of an Overspeed drill can be used to help teach mental toughness, grit, perseverance, and determination.

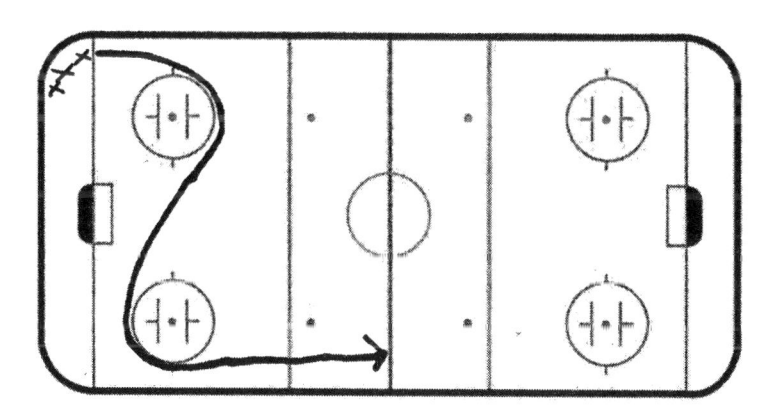

Peanut Drill

The Peanut Drill is a great drill for working on changing direction. It requires two processes to occur. First the player has to stop current momentum in one direction. Second, the player must use explosive fast twitch muscles to move in another. This drill does not require a stop/start change of direction, but rather an ability to move slightly to the right and back to the left and vice versa. That primary change of direction occurs at the hash marks. The Peanut Drill requires athletes to touch the hash marks with their skates before going around the next circle. A lot of times players will try to cheat because it is very difficult to skate full speed and get around the next circle properly. Again, having a coach stand above or below the hash marks helps the athletes properly execute the drill.

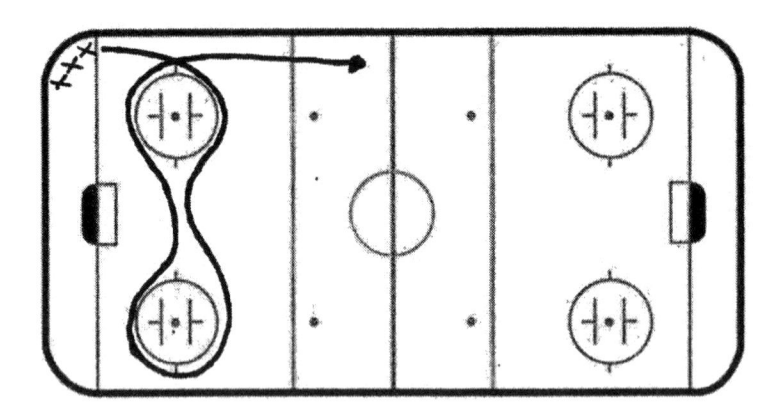

Quick Sprints Drill

The Quick Sprints Drill has idiosyncrasies that require detailed attention. The athletes line up behind the dots in two lines, one behind each circle. When the coach blows the whistle, they must execute a quick start and in very little time will have to execute a proper power turn. After turning, they need to keep their momentum going and sprint as fast as they can through the blue or red lines (depending on where the end of the drill is set). Fast starts are essential in hockey, and in a race as short as this they are equally important. The athletes need to get low and be prepared to explode forward and in as few strides as possible reach the goal line. There, they need to do a power turn. The space is small and they are moving fast. A power turn requires athletes to use their edges. I can't stress this point enough. Often, athletes will use one edge while neglecting the other leg. On a right turn, many athletes will use their inside edge on their left skate. However, on their right leg (the inside leg on the right turn), they will not be able to rotate their outside edge properly. Some hockey players, especially when they are young will lift up their inside leg and glide on the outside one. Most will attempt to keep the right outside edge on the ground, but instead of making a clean cut in the ice, their skates will cause small little divots or choppy cuts in the ice. This slows them down because it causes unnecessary friction with the ice.

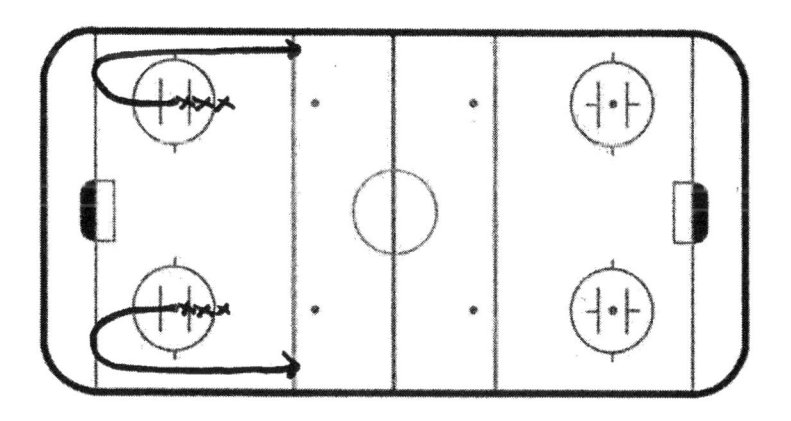

Outside Edge Hold Drill

In this drill we are combining the S Sprint with an outside edge hold around the center circle. As the athletes explode out of the second turn of the S Sprint, they will continue sprinting toward the center circle. Once they reach the circle, they will lift up their outside leg and keep their inside leg on the ice. They will rotate onto their outside edge of the inside leg and skate around the circle. Most athletes when they do this the first time will go around the edge and stand up. They don't stay in a hockey position because the force being exerted on the inside leg is enormous. The player is skating at full speed and to maintain balance and stability on one leg is very difficult. Yet, it helps teach athletes the importance of form. If the athletes execute this properly and can maintain their edges they will go fast around the circle. If they stand up or are not strong enough on their edges, they will slow down. Often, the outside edge will dig into the ice too hard, causing unnecessary friction, and slowing the athletes down. During this drill it is important to have a coach near the middle circle to watch and provide instruction.

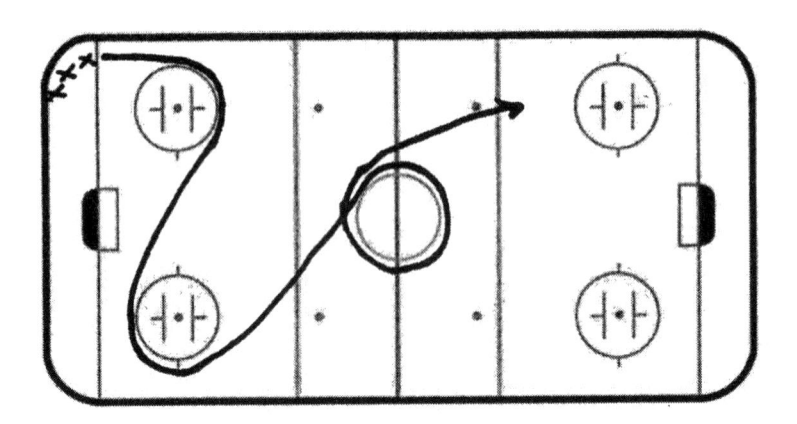

Transition Sprint Drill

This drill works on a forward to backward and backward to forward transition. At the first transition, athletes need to maintain a low and wide base. From that wide base the athletes adjust their edges so they are on the inside part of the blade of the outside leg (in the case of the first transition, the left leg) and on the outside part of the blade of the inside leg (in this case, the right leg). From this wide base, the athletes should in one powerful stride push under, with full blade extension, and with the entire blade on the ice.

In the second transition (near the tops of the circles), the athletes open up, press off the right leg (when opening up to the left) and push forward. Often when the transition is backward, many athletes use four to five crossovers to make the transition and move a few meters. This is a waste of energy. If they are making that many strides, they are standing too tall, not fully extending the stride, and don't have the entire blade on the ice. When opening up to transition forward, it is also important to maintain these principles.

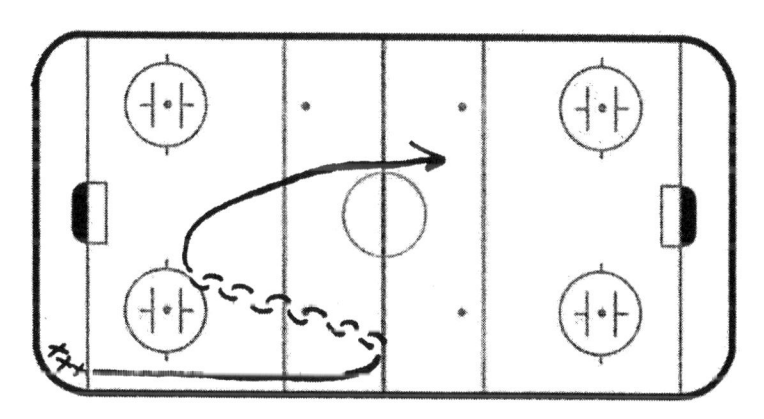

Two Circle Sprint Drill

All the principles about crossing over and the importance of staying low are pertinent here (as they are in every drill). The athletes skate around the circle and explode out of the circle and pick up speed while creating a second larger circle. Athletes will increase their speed throughout much of the drill and it will be important to make sure they stay low the entire time.

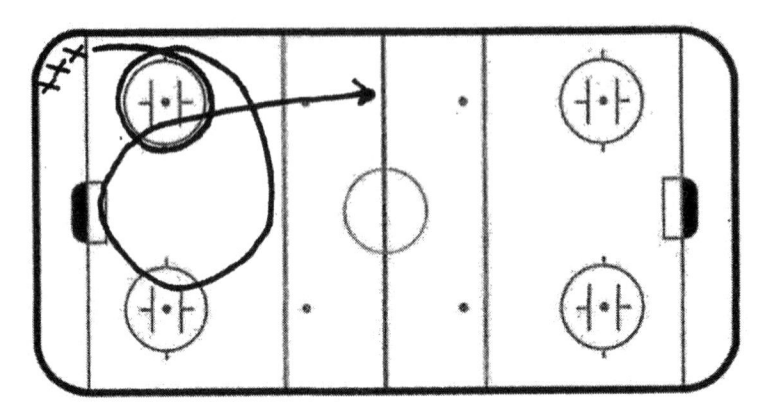

Transition Variation

Same drill as above except this one includes transitions.

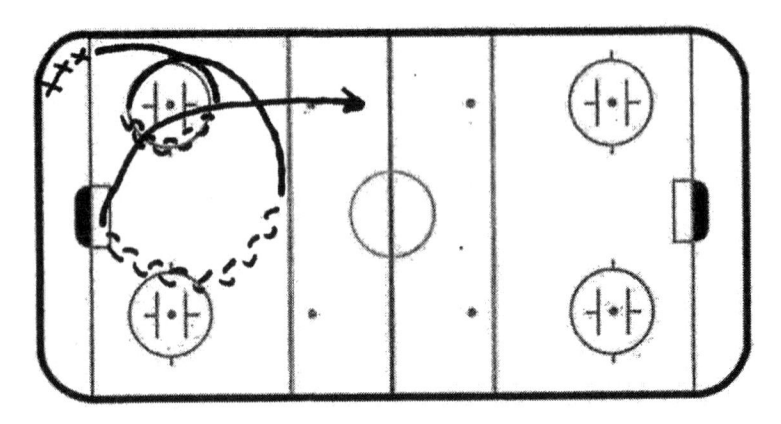

Figure 8 (long version)

In this version of the Figure 8, skaters canvas the entire ice. The turn radius is wide on this drill and allows the athletes the room to really skate very fast. The pressure exerted on the inner leg is less than a tighter circle so the drill lets athletes focus on stride mechanics more than sharpening the turn radius.

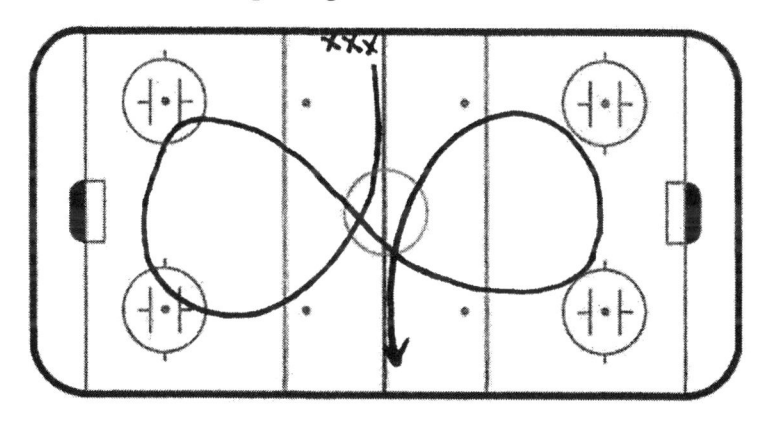

Half-ice Sprint

The Half-Ice Sprint Drill is fun because it introduces competition. The key for the athletes is to skate as fast as possible staying along the boards and making the turn radius as sharp as possible. After skating behind the net, they skate as fast as possible toward the red line. A lot of players aren't strong enough on their skates and their turn radius will take them all the way to the boards.

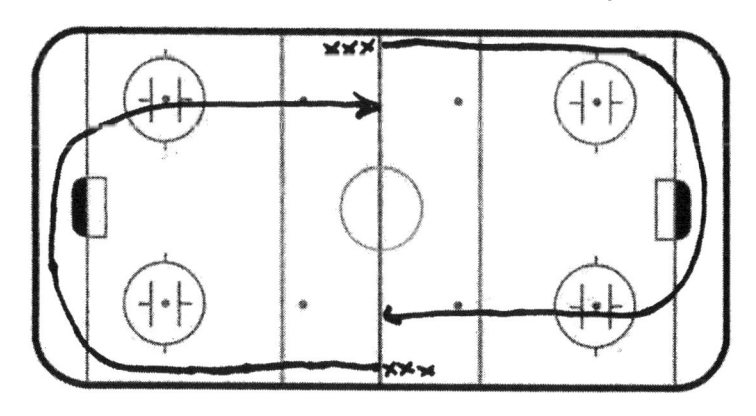

Back check Sprint Drill

The hardest part to teaching Overspeed is to get athletes to skate at truly 100%. This drill adds motivation to skate hard since pucks and scoring are involved. The X's have the pucks and are on offense. The O's are on defense. Depending on the level and any skill differentials, the players adjust the distance between the two skaters starting the drill. For example, if one of the players is much faster than the rest, have that player start much closer on offense and farther on defense. The point isn't so much what happens at the end of the drill, but rather what happens from the start to the far blue. When both athletes skate at 100 percent during the entire drill and push outside their comfort zones, the drill is a success.

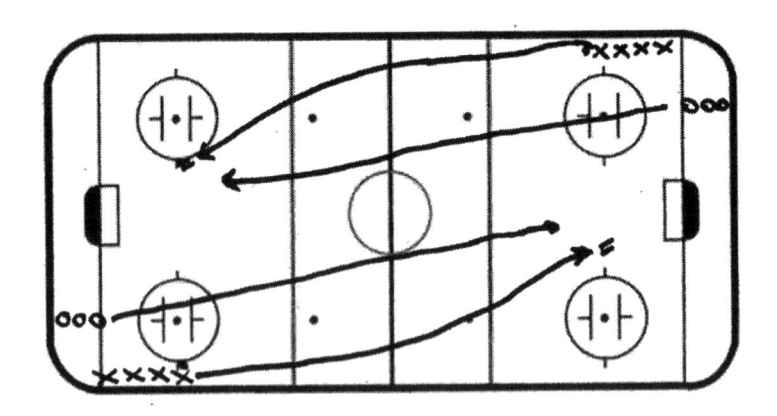

Overspeed with Shooting and Passing

Overspeed with Shooting and Passing uses the same principles already discussed, but now skating with a puck and shooting are added to the drill. The first drill, on the left side of the rink, is a figure 8 shooting drill. When executing this drill, the point is to simulate offensive zone play. Players act as if they have received a pass down low and make their way up the boards. A defensive player makes the offensive player cut quickly toward the boards while protecting the puck. Let's say the defense reacts well this time and so the player makes another quick cut. What does come out of the cut, though, is the most important part of the drill. Often in drills practicing shooting, players will "tee-up" their shots. After getting into position to shoot, they take aim, hold for a second, stop moving their feet, and *then* release. Unfortunately, this is a very bad habit. Practice can certainly hurt a player's performance and development if done this way! The goal is to come out of the figure eight and not stop moving the feet for one second. For defenseman this is very difficult to stop.

In the drill on the right side of the rink, athletes make a quick turn near the face-off dot, churn their feet to the blue, and perform crossovers to center ice and into the slot. Athletes should never stop moving their feet, like the previous drill, and should shoot the puck while moving their feet.

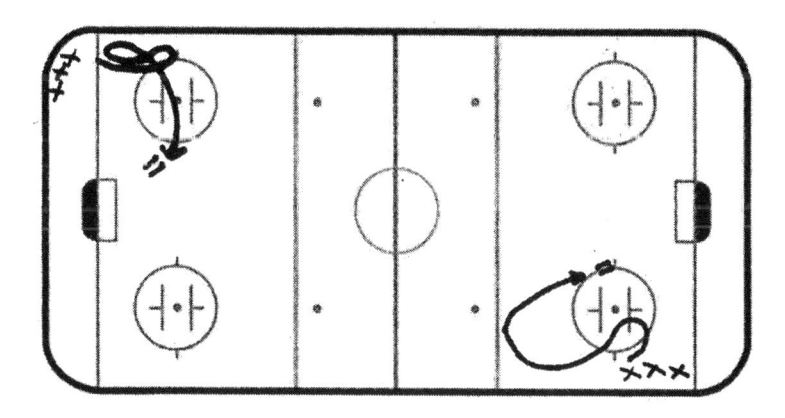

More Shooting Drills

These two drills are easy, but effective. The first one, on the left side of the rink, requires a coach near the hash marks toward the middle of the ice. As players turn around the top of the circle at top speed, they'll have a tendency to hold the puck too long before shooting. If this happens, a coach needs to simulate a defenseman and pressure the shooter to shoot.

In the second drill, on the right side of the rink, the players perform a tight weave at the top of the circles. Right handed shooters can either shoot off their backhands or will need to come around the cone to shoot on the forehand. In either case, it is imperative the shot gets off right away and certainly before the hash marks.

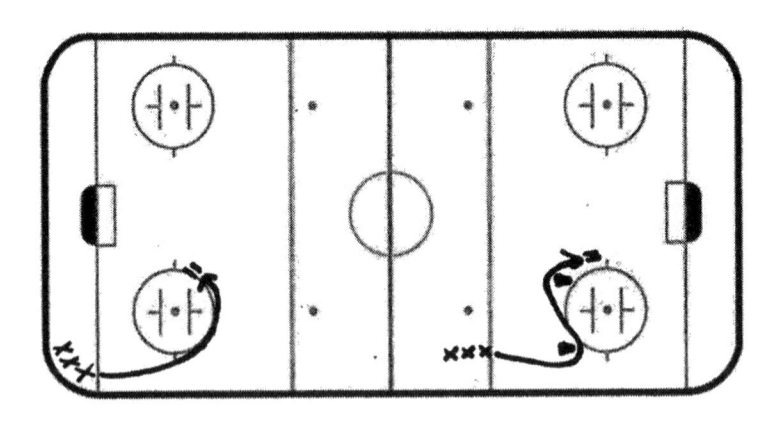

Pass, Receive, and Shoot Drills

The drill that starts at the red line (mid ice) here is a quick start drill. The player explodes to the center of the ice, turns, catches the pass, and quickly skates into the slot and shoots. It looks like the shooter should have plenty of time, but at full speed it is a matter of perhaps a second or two from the time the players catch the puck until they shoot. In this drill, the players should shoot the puck by the top of the circles. The hash marks are far too low for this drill. In the second drill, the players are working on passing while moving. Players take off with the puck, power turn and pass it back to the second player in line. The entire time the players continue to move their feet until they get open. The players should catch the puck and release it as fast as possible.

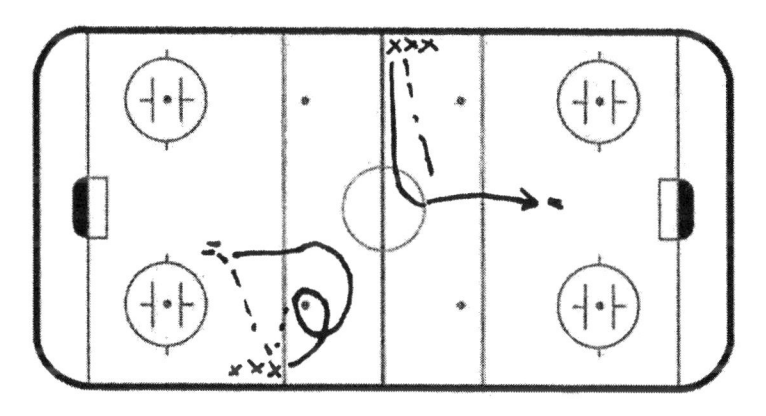

Cycle and Shoot Drill & Center Ice Figure 8 Drill

The Overspeed drill that starts at center ice is working on passing. The key to this drill is to make sure the athletes never stop moving their feet. As they come around the turns, athletes have a tendency to stop moving their feet in anticipation of the pass. Coaches need to consistently re-enforce this principle The drill diagramed on the right side of the rink below helps highlight how important it is to maintain standards and execute properly. While the drill appears simple and brief, there are several key elements. Most athletes will round the top of the circle at a relatively slow pace. As the puck travels toward the athlete, the athlete will stop moving his or her feet. Once the skater catches the puck, he or she will look up, pause, and then shoot. In a real game this rarely, if ever, happens. It is imperative to move at full speed around the circle, catch the pass with the feet moving, and shoot the puck immediately.

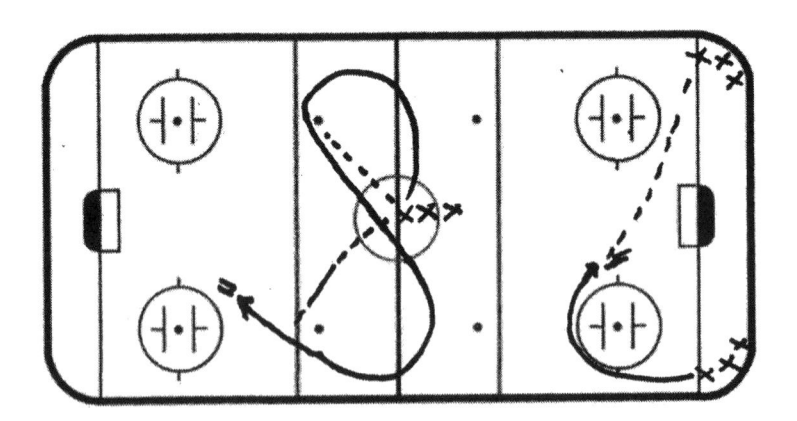

Agility Shooting Drill & Circle Pass/Shoot Drill

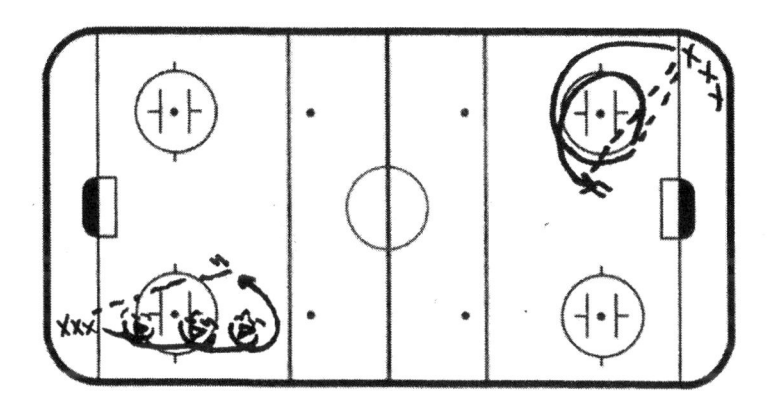

    The drill, diagramed above on the left side of the rink, focuses more on skating than shooting, and is a good one for agility purposes. Athletes have to conduct quick transitions around the cones (as tight as possible) and after the last cone churn their feet toward the slot.

    In the second drill diagramed, the athletes can either start with the puck or not. As they turn around the circle, they will pass the puck to the second player in line – or alternatively, receive and pass back a puck from the second player. They continue to churn their feet around the circle and catch a pass from the second player and shoot. It is easy, and most effective, when done at high speeds.

Underspeed Training

The opposite of Overspeed Training is Underspeed Training. The concept is just as the name suggests. Instead of trying to push athletes to go beyond their comfort zone so as to train their muscles to go faster, they are told to slow down. In Underspeed Training athletes focus on full extension of the stride, full blade on the ice, and proper skating posture. Only two drills are detailed below, but any drill that is used for Overspeed can be used for Underspeed. However, some Underspeed drills don't make for very good Overspeed drills because they are too long. Underspeed drills can be performed for extended periods of time since the athlete is not skating at 100 percent.

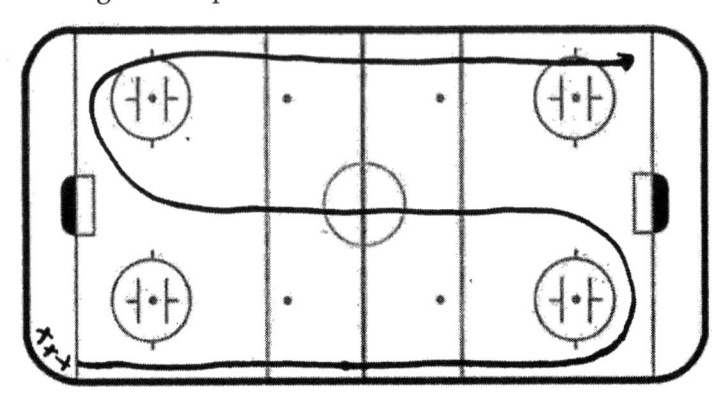

During Overspeed drills it is important coaches are placed throughout the drill to give the athletes constant direction. For many hockey players, there is a *great difference between how they are skating and how they perceive themselves as skating*. They might think they are low and in a proper skating stride when really they are off 20 or 30 degrees or more. This happens because the closer the skater gets to the hockey position, the tougher it gets on the legs. The lower position is always more exhausting, although from this position an athlete can skate faster and quicker. Also, when hockey players are trying to get low, sometimes they will bring their chest to the ice instead of bending their knees. This is largely because bending at the knees is so much more difficult. The drill pictured here is a long Underspeed drill. It covers a lot of ice and allows coaches to stand at the bottom of the circles and at center ice. Coaches can place their stick just above the height that a player should be at if in a proper position to help remind players to stay low.

The other large two circle drill is nice because athletes work on crossovers and emphasize pushing all the way through with their inside leg. Placing coaches at the corners is best since this is where it is hardest to maintain a proper crossover.

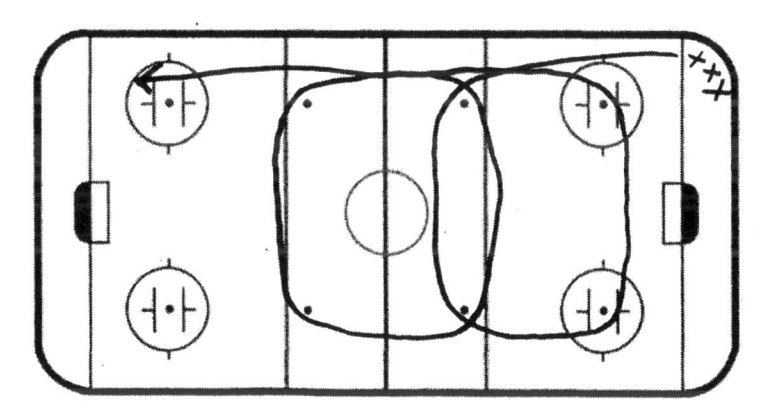

When athletes have passed puberty it is safe to use weight vests during Underspeed Training. Doing so helps athletes work on developing the necessary strength and stability in the leg and butt muscles to be able to stay in a proper skating position.

Agility Training: Sample Drills

Chapter 5

The Square Drill

At the starting position sprint forward to the first cone, pivot to a shuffle, pivot to a backward sprint at the second cone, transition to a shuffle at the third cone, and transition forward at the fourth/starting cone and sprint through the first cone to finish the drill.

There are two very important points to understand when doing this agility drill. First, athletes should attempt to make as clean of cuts around the cones as possible. Instead of sprinting forward and making a clean transition to a lateral shuffle, many athletes will round out around the cone. The goal, however, should be to make a 90 degree cut around the cone. This is a more athletic movement and requires greater body control, stability, and strength. One the ice, if a player is in the corner and is trying to shake off a defender, a rounded change of direction will allow the defender time to react. If the player can cut quickly, defending the offensive player becomes much harder.

During the final sprint the pivot motion is critical. The athlete should lateral shuffle till he or she gets past the final cone and then sprint forward (leaning forward and getting good acceleration).

Variations: There are almost an infinite amount of variations for any agility drill. An athlete can do karaoke or other lateral movement variations on left-to-right and right-to-left movements.

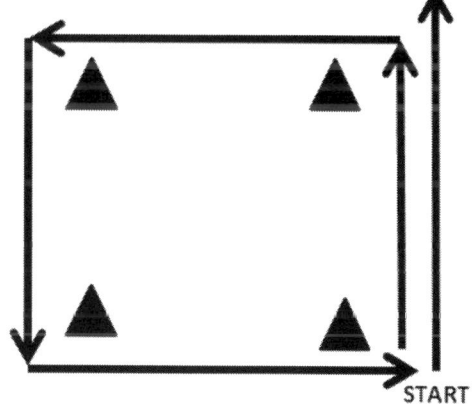

Pro-Agility

This is one of my favorite agility drills to do because it can become very competitive. Two athletes can race each other by starting on opposites sides of the cone. One athlete will stand on one side of the center cone and the other athlete on the other. Each will sprint toward the first cone (can be either cone), then sprint to the far cone on the other side before returning to the middle. This drill requires a very tangible and necessary skill – the ability to completely stop one's momentum in one direction, and reversing the momentum in the completely opposite direction. In the Square Drill, for example, an athlete can maintain some speed when going around the cones, especially on the last turn. However, in this drill the athlete actually has to stop forward progress and reverse direction. It's not easy to do, but very valuable. The start on this drill is also important. Athletes should face each other and get low. When the whistle blows, they need to drive toward the first cone, staying low, and leaning into the sprint. When they get to the end cones, they should be low. The more upright they are, the harder it is to be explosive. Since this drill is about short 1-3 second sprints, the athletes should be working on quick starts. Each athlete performs 3 quick starts in each drill.

Distance between cones 5-15 meters

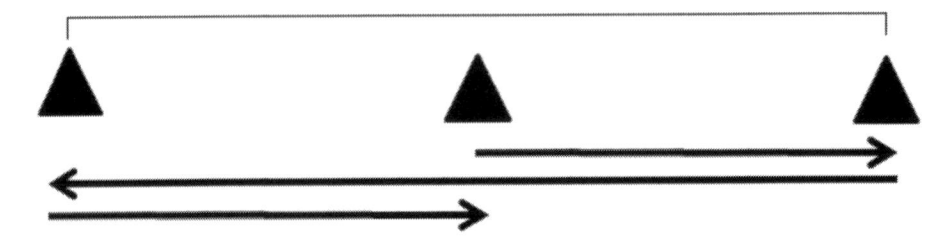

The Mimic Drill

The Mimic Drill is a great drill to work on athleticism because it is less structured. Structured drills like Pro-Agility are great drills and they help develop quick feet skills. However, they are missing one element of athleticism that is important to train – the ability to read and react to an opposing player. A hockey player isn't given commands on the ice, told when to cut, when to pivot, and when to transition. Those drills that tell the athlete exactly what to do and when to do it are still important and beneficial. They are especially great for practicing footwork, becoming more agile, and getting quicker. The Mimic Drill is great because it provides a level of uncertainty that all team sports have.

In this drill, all you need is a line. Two players stand on either side of the line and face each other. One player is offense and the other is defense. The offensive player looks to evade the defensive player by changing direction and sprinting up and down the line. The defensive player attempts to mimic the movements of the offensive player, always staying in front of him. It's a tiring drill. Sets of ten or less seconds can be used, but ample rest is, as always, of the utmost importance.

```
           | Player 1 - Offense |
━━━━━━━━━━━━━━━━━━━━━━━━━━━━━━━━━━━━━━━━
           | Player 2 - Defense |
```

The Zig-Zag Drill

Sprint to the nearest cone, plant, pivot, and sprint to the next nearest cone. An athlete can pivot two ways. The first way is forward, as if the athlete is playing offense. The player running toward a cone on the right will pivot left. The second way is as a defensive player. In this variation of the drill, the athlete acts as a mirror to the offensive player who is zig-zagging through the drill. The athlete wants to keep the imaginary offensive player in front of him or her and so should pivot toward the offensive player every time. For example, if running toward a cone on the right side of this drill the athlete will pivot right.

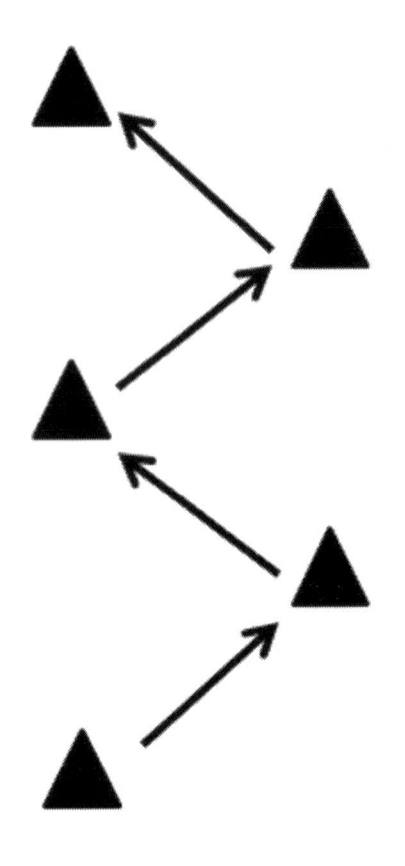

When doing this drill, one of the most important concepts to understand is the importance of the pivot. This forces an athlete to slow momentum in one direction and apply it in another. To do so effectively, the athlete must get low and plant the foot firmly, stopping momentum toward the cone, and then exploding off this foot toward the next cone. Most athletes tend to lack sufficient knee-bend when performing pivots.

1 v 1 Unstructured Agility Drill

Player 2 (defense) sprints forward to a line marked on the floor. The exact distance will depend on the speed of the athletes and if there are any talent differentials between the two. Player 1 (offense) will sprint forward as soon as Player 2 hits the line starting the drill. Player 2 starts to back-peddle as fast as possible after touching the line. The goal of Player 2 is to keep player 1 in front and to not allow Player 1 to get around him or her. Another aspect to the drill is to imagine that the net is at the end of the drill, in the center, somewhere between 25-35 meters away. Player 2 is acting just as a player would on ice – keep the offensive player in front or away from the center. Player 1 obviously wants to get around Player 2 and can use a variety of strategies. The depiction of this drill only has one pivot, but there should be more than one pivot or change of direction if the athletes are equally matched.

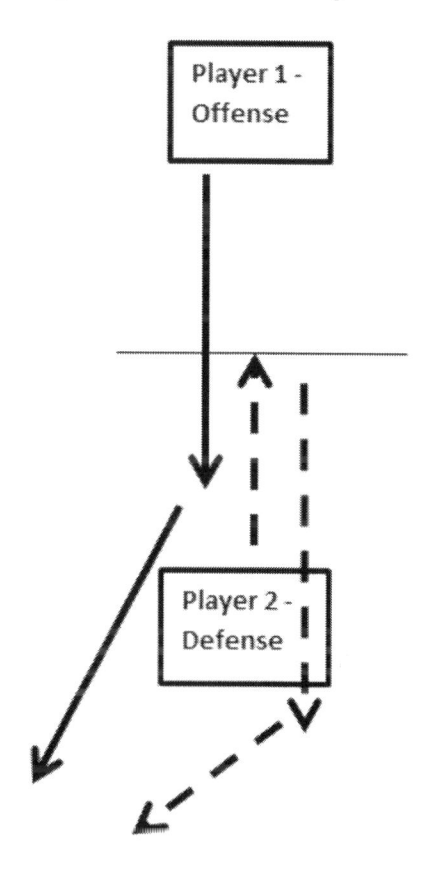

Quick Feet Transitions

Each cone should be about five meters apart. The athlete starts slightly to one side of the cones and sprints as fast as possible to the first cone, quickly transitions around it, and sprints to the next. The athlete should repeat this until the drill is finished. An athlete may want to use up to five cones in this drill, but should make sure not to use too many. Remember, building up lactic acid will reduce the ability of the athlete to train at 100 percent. When going around each cone, cut laterally, backward, laterally, and then forward. The athlete should always face the direction that he or she began the drill.

This drill is extremely important for building foot speed and coordination. It requires a lot of fine-tuned athleticism to get around a tiny cone quickly. After making the transition out of the cone, it is important that the athlete drive forward, leaning a little into the sprint to the next cone. The acceleration out of the cone is extremely important.

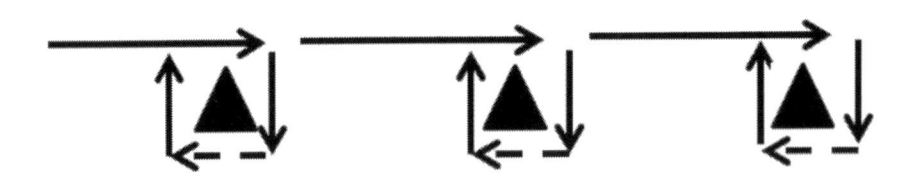

The L-Drill

The L-Drill is another simple agility drill that requires an athlete to be able to accelerate and decelerate quickly. The value of this skill in hockey is very important. The athlete starts the drill next to the top cone on the left side. He can start backward or forward. For the sake of explaining the drill, let's suppose the athlete sprints forward to the bottom cone. The athlete must shuffle quickly across the length of that cone and sprint backwards back to the starting cone. This drill can either be done one repetition at a time or done for a specified amount of time (10 seconds is ideal).

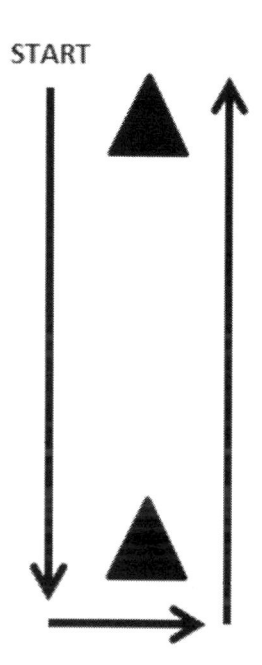

The Four Cone Quick Reaction Drill

The Four Cone Quick Reaction Drill is a great way to introduce some variation and quick thinking into an agility training session. The athlete starts in the middle. The coach yells out a number (1 through 4) and the athlete must react to the number being called, sprint to that cone, touch it, and sprint back to the middle.

Acceleration/Deceleration Drill

In the Acceleration/Deceleration Drill the athlete starts at the cone on the far left and sprints forward to each cone as fast as possible. The athlete comes to a complete stop. After stopping, he or she gets low and accelerates to the next cone. The distance between each cone is about five to eight meters. The goal of this drill is to help the athlete learn how to control his or her body and come to complete stops after accelerating.

Variation: At each cone the athlete can work on acceleration and deceleration without coming to a complete stop. The athlete can accelerate and slow down to perhaps 50 percent speed at the cone and re-accelerate.

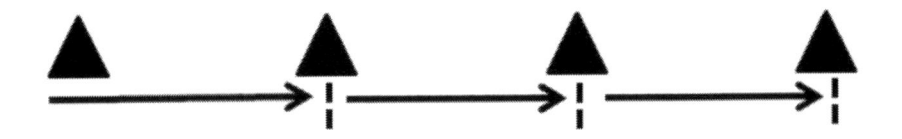

END NOTES

[1] Belluck, Pam. "Parents Try to Reclaim Their Children's Time." New York Times 13 June 2000, n. pag. Web. 4 Jan. 2013. <http://www.nytimes.com/2000/06/13/us/parents-try-to-reclaim-their-children-s-time.html?pagewanted=all&src=pm>.

[2] Ibid.

[3] Levine, Joshua. "Hockey Parent Survey". www.thefortisacademy.com. 20 April 2012. Web.

[4] Ibid.

[5] Ibid.

[6] "Intensive Training and Sports Specialization in Young Athletes." Pediatrics: Official Journal of the American Academy of Pediatrics. 106.1 (2000): 154-157. Print. <http://pediatrics.aappublications.org/content/106/1/154.full.pdf>.

[7] National Association for Sport and Physical Education. (2010). Guidelines for participation in youth sports programs: Specialization versus multi-sport participation [Position statement]. Reston, VA: Author.

[8] "Minnesota Made 2013 Hockey Clinics." Minnesota Made. Web. 4 Jan 2013. <http://www.minnesotamadehockey.com/page/show/68535-minnesota-made-2012-hockey-clinics>.

[9] "New Types of Overuse Injuries to Youth Gymnasts' Arms, Wrists And Hands Cause for Concern, Study says." Moms Team. N.p., 01 2008. Web. 4 Jan 2013. <http://www.momsteam.com/sports/new-types-of-overuse-injuries-to-youth-gymnasts-arms-wrists-and-hands-cause-for-concern-study>.

[10] Ibid.

[11] Bardi, Jason. "Medical Imaging Shows Gymnasts Sustain More Types of Injuries than Previously Thought." The American Association of Physicists in Medicine. N.p., 12 2008. Web. 4 Jan 2013. <http://www.aapm.org/meetings/rsna08/story4.asp>.

[12] "Long-Term Athlete Development." USA Hockey. USA Hockey. Web. 4 Jan 2013. <http://www.usahockey.com/ADMKids_10Factors.asp>

[13] Baker, Joseph, and Jean Cote. "Shifting Training Requirements During Athlete Development: Deliberate Practice, Deliberate Play and Other Sport Involvement in the Acquisition of Sport Expertise." Essential Processes for Attaining Peak Performance. Hackfort, Dieter and Gershon Tenenbaum. New York: Meyer & Meyer Sport, 2006. 104. Online.

[14] Ibid.

[15] Mitchell, Stephen, Judith Oslin, and Linda Griffin. Teaching Sport Concepts and Skills: A Tractical Games Approach. 2nd Ed. Champaign, IL: Human Kinetics, 2006. 22. Web.

[16] "Wellness to World Cup: Long Term Player Development." Canada Soccer. Canada Soccer Association, n.d. Web. 4 Jan 2013. <http://www.canadasoccer.com/files/CSA_2009_WellnessWorldCup_volume1_EN.pdf>.
[17] Ibid.
[18] Blatherwick, Jack. "The myth of leaving home and advancing quickly." . N.p.. Web. 4 Jan 2013. <http://www.asha.pointstreaksites.com/files/uploaded_documents/74/MHCA_-_2010_Jack_Blatherwich_AdvancingQuickly.pdf>.
[19] Ibid.
[20] Micheli, Lyle. "Overuse Injuries in Youth Sports." . Children's Hospital Boston and Harvard Medical School, n.d. Web. 4 Jan 2013. <http://childrenshospital.org/clinicalservices/Site1172/Documents/overuseinjuries.pdf>.
[21] Ibid.
[22] "Stop Sports Injuries Campaign." Stop Sports Injuries. Stop Sports Injuries. Web. 4 Jan 2013. <http://www.stopsportsinjuries.org/media.asp>
[23] Ibid.
[24] American Orthopaedic Society for Sports EMB. "Dramatic Increase In "Tommy John" Surgery In Young Athlete Patients Cause For Concern." Medical News Today. MediLexicon, Intl., 12 Jul. 2008. Web. 4 Jan. 2013. <http://www.medicalnewstoday.com/releases/113854.php>
[25] Ibid.
[26] Hyman, Mark. "A Children's Crusade." Sports Illustrated. 07 2010: n. page. Web. 4 Jan. 2013. <http://sportsillustrated.cnn.com/vault/article/magazine/MAG1170192/index.htm>.
[27] Reynolds, Gretchen. "A New Breed of Knee Injury in Young Athletes." Well. New York Times, 26 2011. Web. Web. 4 Jan. 2013. <http://well.blogs.nytimes.com/2011/10/26/a-new-breed-of-knee-injury-in-young-athletes/>.
[28] Ibid.
[29] Ibid.
[30] Hyman, Mark. Until It Hurts: America's obsession with youth sports and how it harms our kids. Boston: Beacon Press, 2009. 70. Print.
[31] Hyman, Mark. Until It Hurts: America's obsession with youth sports and how it harms our kids. Boston: Beacon Press, 2009. 71. Print.
[32] The Arthritis Foundation. Sports Injuries Put Youth at Risk – Arthritis Foundation Spreading Awareness for June as "Sports Injury Prevention" Month. http://www.pr.com/press-release/330442. Web.

[33] Kelly, Jack. "Does ACL Surgery Cause Arthritis? UPMC Team Seeks Answers." Post Gazette [Pittsburgh] 29 MARCH 2012, n. pag. Web. 4 Jan. 2013. <http://www.post-gazette.com/stories/news/health/does-acl-surgery-cause-arthritis-upmc-team-seeks-answers-275375/>.
[34] Ibid.
[35] Sun, Rebecca. Sports Illustrated Kids. 23 DEC 2010: 51-54. Web. 5 Jan. 2013. <http://www.stopsportsinjuries.org/files/pdf/news_release_dec23.pdf>.
[36] Gould, Daniel. Early Sport Specialization: A Psychological Perspective, Journal of Physical Education, Recreation & Dance; Oct. 2010; 81, 8.
[37] Eric, Duhatschek. "The Great One's message to parents: Let your kids have fun." Globe and Mail [Calgary] 26 SEP 2008, A3. Web. 7 Jan. 2013. <http://www.hockeymanitoba.ca/docs/Gretzky-Globe and Mail.pdf>.
[38] "Long-Term Athlete Development." USA Hockey. USA Hockey. Web. 4 Jan 2013. <http://www.usahockey.com/ADMKids_10Factors.asp>
[39] Lazar, Kay. "Teens training too hard, too often: Athlete's injuries concern doctors." Boston Globe 01 JUN 2010, n. pag. Web. 7 Jan. 2013. <http://www.boston.com/news/science/articles/2010/06/01/young_athletes_injuries_on_the_rise/?page=2>.
[40] Susan, Knapp. "Researchers: No harm in learning two languages." Dartmouth News 04 NOV 2002, n. pag. Web. 7 Jan. 2013. <http://www.dartmouth.edu/~news/releases/2002/nov/110402a.html>.
[41] "Cognitive Benefits of Learning Language." American Council on the Teaching of Foreign Languages. N.p.. Web. 7 Jan 2013. <http://www.actfl.org/advocacy/discover-languages/advocacy/discover-languages/advocacy/discover-languages/resources-8?pageid=4724>.
[42] Vaeyens, Roel, Arne Gullich, Chelsea Warr, and Renaat Philippaerts. "Talent identification and promotion programmes of Olympic athletes." Journal of Sports Sciences. 27.13 (2009): 1367-1380. Web. 7 Jan. 2013. <http://www.tandfonline.com/doi/abs/10.1080/02640410903110974>.
[43] Breener, Joel. "Overuse Injuries, Overtraining, and Burnout in Child and Adolescent Athletes." Pediatrics. 119.6 (2007): 1242-1245. Web. 7 Jan. 2013. <http://pediatrics.aappublications.org/content/119/6/1242.full>.
[44] Moesch, Karen, A.-M. Elbe, M.-L. T. Hauge, and J. M. Wikman. "Late specialization: the key to success in centimeters, grams, or seconds (cgs) sports." Scandinavian Journal of Medicine & Science in Sports. (2011): e282-e290. Print.
[45] Hyman, Mark. Until It Hurts: America's obsession with youth sports and how it harms our kids. Boston: Beacon Press, 2009. 20-21. Print.

[46] Wall, Michael, and Jean Cote. "Developmental activities that lead to dropout and investment in sport." Physical Education and Sport Pedagogy. 12.1 (2007): 77-87. Print.

[47] Soberlak, Peter, and Jean Cote. "The Developmental Activities of Elite Ice Hockey Players." Journal of Applied Sport Psychology. 15. (2003): 41-49. Print.

[48] Ericsson, K. Anders. "The Influence of Experience and Deliberate Practice on the Development of Superior Expert Performance". The Cambridge Handbook of Expertise and Expert Performance. Ericsson, K. Anders, Charness, Neil, Feltovich, Paul J., and Robert Hoffman. New York: Cambridge University Press. 2006. 688. Online.

[49] Gladwell, Malcom. Outliers: The Story of Success. 1st ed. New York: Little, Brown, and Company, 2008. 39. Print.

[50] Ibid.

[51] Ibid. Pages 41-42.

[52] Ericsson, K. Anders. "The Influence of Experience and Deliberate Practice on the Development of Superior Expert Performance". The Cambridge Handbook of Expertise and Expert Performance. Ericsson, K. Anders, Charness, Neil, Feltovich, Paul J., and Robert Hoffman. New York: Cambridge University Press. 2006. 691. Online.

[53] Cote, Jean, Ronnie Lidor, and Dieter Hackfort. "ISSP Position Stand: To sample or to specialize? Seven postulates about youth sport activities that lead to continued participation and elite performance." International Journal of Sport and Exercise Psychology. 9. (2009): 7-17. Web. 7 Jan. 2013. <http://www.issponline.org/documents/positionstand2009-1.pdf>.

[54] Gulbin, Jason. Why Deliberate Practice Isn't Enough. Dimensions of Performance Symposium. September 2006, Berlin, Germany. Print.

[55] Anderson, Gregory, and Peter Twist. "Trainability of Children." Idea Fitness. (2005): n. page. Print.

[56] Ibid.

[57] Gladwell, Malcom. Outliers: The Story of Success. 1st ed. New York: Little, Brown, and Company, 2008. 38. Print.

[58] Ericsson, K. Anders. "The Influence of Experience and Deliberate Practice on the Development of Superior Expert Performance". The Cambridge Handbook of Expertise and Expert Performance. Ericsson, K. Anders, Charness, Neil, Feltovich, Paul J., and Robert Hoffman. New York: Cambridge University Press. 2006. 700. Online.

[59] Vaeyens, Roel, Arne Gullich, Chelsea Warr, and Renaat Philippaerts. "Talent identification and promotion programmes of Olympic athletes." Journal of Sports Sciences. 27.13 (2009): 1367-1380. Web. 7 Jan. 2013. <http://www.tandfonline.com/doi/abs/10.1080/02640410903110974>.

[60] Ibid.

[61] Cote, Jean and Bruce Abernethy. "A Developmental Approach to Sport Expertise." The Oxford Handbook of Sport and Performance Psychology. Murphy, Shane. Oxford: Oxford University Press. 2012. 436. Online.

[62] Barreiros, Andre, Jean Cote, and Antonio Manuel Fonseca. "From early to adult sport success: Analyzing athletes' progression in national squads." European Journal of Sport Science. (2012): 1-5. Print.

[63] "Choice League Mite's Home Page." Minnesota Made. Minnesota MAde. Web. 7 Jan 2013. <http://www.minnesotamadehockey.com/page/show/179303-choice-mite-s-home-page>.

[64] Cote, Jean and Bruce Abernethy. "A Developmental Approach to Sport Expertise." The Oxford Handbook of Sport and Performance Psychology. Murphy, Shane. Oxford: Oxford University Press. 2012. 436. Online.

[65] Gladwell, Malcom. Outliers: The Story of Success. 1st ed. New York: Little, Brown, and Company, 2008. 22-23. Print.

[66] Levine, Joshua. "Hockey Parent Survey". www.thefortisacademy.com. 20 April 2012. Web.

[67] Ibid.

[68] "Estimated Probability of Competing in Athletics Beyond the High School Interscholastic Level." NCAA . NCAA Research, n.d. Web. 8 Jan 2013. <http://fs.ncaa.org/Docs/eligibility_center/Athletics_Information/Probability_of_Competing_Past_High_School.pdf>.

[69] Keegan, Tom. "Strictly By The Numbers." Hockey Center. N.p.. Web. 8 Jan 2013. <http://www.hockeycenter.com/index_college_men.htm>.

[70] Bowen, William G., and James L. Shulman. The Game of Life: College Sports and Educational Values. Princeton, NJ: Princeton University Press, 2001. 64. Print.

[71] Ibid.

[72] Ibid. Page 159.

[73] Ibid. Page 161.

[74] Jill, Lieber Steeg, Jodi Upton, Patrick Bohn, and Steve Berkowitz. "College athletes studies guided toward 'major in eligibilit'y." USA Today 19 NOV 2008, n. pag. Web. 8 Jan. 2013. <http://usatoday30.usatoday.com/sports/college/2008-11-18-majors-cover_N.htm>.

[75] Ibid.

[76] "Estimated Probability of Competing in Athletics Beyond the High School Interscholastic Level." NCAA . NCAA Research, n.d. Web. 8 Jan 2013. <http://fs.ncaa.org/Docs/eligibility_center/Athletics_Information/Probability_of_Competing_Past_High_School.pdf>.

[77] Ibid.
[78] Campell, Ken. "Just how tough is it to reach the NHL?." ESPN NHL. ESPN, 13 2007. Web. 8 Jan 2013.
<http://sports.espn.go.com/nhl/news/story?page=campbell1113>.
[79] Russo, John. "The last of community-based hockey." Let's Play Hockey. 27 2012: n. page. Web. 8 Jan. 2013. <www.letsplayhockey.com/online-edition/russo/932-the-last-of-community-based-hockey.html>.
[80] "Choice League Mite's Home Page." Minnesota Made. Minnesota MAde. Web. 7 Jan 2013.
<http://www.minnesotamadehockey.com/page/show/179303-choice-mite-s-home-page>.
[81] Ibid.
[82] Mayo Clinic Staff, . "Strength Training: OK for Kids?." Mayo Clinic. Mayo Clinic, 18 2012. Web. 8 Jan 2013.
<http://www.mayoclinic.com/health/strength-training/HQ01010/NSECTIONGROUP=2>.
[83] Ibid.
[84] Anderson, Gregory, and Peter Twist. "Trainability of Children." Idea Fitness. (2005): n. page. Print.
[85] Burd, Nicholas A., Richard J. Andrews, Daniel W.D. West, et al. "Muscle time under tension during resistance exercise stimulates differential muscle protein sub-fractional synthetic responses in men." Journal of Physiology. 590.2 (2012): 351-362. Print.
[86] Lehrer, Jonah. "Measurements That Mislead: From the SAT to the NFL, the problem with short-term tests." Wall Street Journal [New York City] 02 APR 2011, n. pag. Web. 15 Jan. 2013.
<http://online.wsj.com/article/SB10001424052748704471904576230931647955902.html>.
[87] Meers, Kevin. "Does the NFL Combine Matter: Defense." The Harvard College Sports Analysis Collective. N.p., 28 FEB 2012. Web. Web. 15 Jan. 2013. <http://harvardsportsanalysis.wordpress.com/2012/02/28/does-the-nfl-combine-matter-defense/>.
[88] Meers, Kevin. "Does the NFL Combine Matter: Offense." The Harvard College Sports Analysis Collective. N.p., 27 FEB 2012. Web. Web. 15 Jan. 2013. <http://harvardsportsanalysis.wordpress.com/2012/02/27/does-the-nfl-combine-matter-offense/>.
[89] Blatherwick, Jack. "FlexxCoach." "Speed of Mind". N.p.. Web. 15 Jan 2013.
<http://www.flexxcoach.com/learningcenter/resources/cc_NHLCA_Blatherwick_SpeedOfMind.pdf>.

[90] Adam Zajac, Ryszard Jarzabek, and Zbigniew Waskiewicz, "The Diagnostic Value of the 10- and 30-second Wingate Test for Competitive Athletes", Journal of Strength and Conditioning Research 13(1), 16-19

[91] Blatherwick, Jack. OVERSPEED: Skill Training for Hockey. 49. Web. <http://burnsvillehockey.com/DevOverspeed.html>.

[92] "Athletics A Substitute for War: Dr. Walter B. Cannon of Harvard Says Physical Contests Will Provide Outlet for Warlike Emotions." New York Times 25 APR 1915, n. pag. Web. 15 Jan. 2013. <http://query.nytimes.com/mem/archive-free/pdf?res=F0091FFD3C5D17738DDDAC0A94DC405B858DF1D3>.

[93] Ibid.

[94] Jonsson, Patrik. "High school athletics under a microscope." Christian Science Monitor [Boston] 01 APR 2003, n. pag. Web. 17 Jan. 2013. <http://www.csmonitor.com/2003/0401/p17s01-lepr.html>.

[95] Ibid.

[96] Wooden, John, perf. John Wooden: Values, Victory, and Peace of Mind. 2003. Web. 17 Jan 2013. <http://www.hulu.com/watch/303228>.

[97] Rath, T., and D. O. Clifton. How Full is Your Bucket?. New York: Gallup Pr, 2004. Print.

[98] Ibid.

[99] Ibid.

[100] Ibid

[101] Power, F. Clark. "Study documents ethical problems in youth sports." University of Notre Dame. N.p., 28 NOV 2005. Web. 20 Jul 2013. <http://al.nd.edu/news/12416-study-documents-ethical-problems-in-youth-sports/>.

[102] "Quotation Collection." John Wooden Quotes. N.p.. Web. 5 May 2013. <http://www.quotationcollection.com/author/John-Wooden/quotes>.

[103] Carnegie, Dale. How to Win Friends & Influence People. Special Anniversary Edition. New York: Pocket Books, 1936. Print.

Made in the USA
Lexington, KY
17 November 2016